KETO COOKING
FOR *COOL DUDES*

Quick, easy, and delicious keto-friendly meals that will make you smarter, more athletic, and more attractive

BRAD KEARNS
& BRIAN McANDREW

Keto Cooking for Cool Dudes

Quick, easy, and delicious keto-friendly meals that will make you smarter, more athletic, and more attractive

Library of Congress Control Number: 2019908357
Paperback ISBN: 978-1-7326745-2-3 eBook ISBN: 978-1-7326745-3-0
Publisher: Bradventures LLC
Please contact the publisher at bradventuresLLC@gmail.com with any questions, concerns or feedback, and to obtain quantity discounts.

Editor: N/A (first draft was perfect)
Proofreading and Indexing: Tim Tate (indexing@warwick.net)
Art Director and Book Design: Caroline DeVita (CarolineDeVita.com)
Cover photo and Dudes cooking photos: Natalie Brenner (NatalieBrennerPhoto.com)
Muppet artist: Maria Watts (Instagram @doubleshotwatts)
Cute kid in the cover photo: Vanessa McAndrew (Instagram @WholeDoods)
Recipe photos, testing, and inspiration: Sarah Steffens (savorandfancy.com)
Recipe photos on pages 39, 44, 45, 67, 78, 89, 110-115, 126, 181, 198, 204: Dolores Lusitana (situationbook.com)
Fabulous kitchen hostess at her fabulous kitchen: Heidi Bell, Portland, OR
Set design and key grip: Grace McAndrew
Stock photos: Josh Willink, Gregory Pappas, Ekrulila, Rawpixel
Other photos: Steven "eWildlife Photo" Kobrine, Brian McAndrew, Grace McAndrew, Brad Kearns, Tom Cruise, Brad Pitt, Pete Buddha Judge, Hicham El Guerrouj, Wayde van Niekerk, Dwayne "The Rock" Johnson, Mark E. Mark

Printed in the U.S.A.

ACCOLADES FROM FAMOUS PEOPLE FOR KETO COOKING FOR COOL DUDES

"My comeback to win the 2019 Masters—the greatest comeback in the history of sports—is thanks to the white balls that I play with, and white balls that I eat from this cookbook, *Keto Cooking for Cool Dudes*."

—*Tiger Woods*, Champion Golfer of All-Time

"Every morning I have an egg white omelet for breakfast. Seriously. Because my handlers and I don't know any better. Don't be like me. Read the book, man!"

—*LeBron James*, Los Angeles Lakers basketball legend

"We highly recommend this book, and these dudes"

— YHM (YOUNG, HOT MILLENNIALS) BOOK CLUB, Portland, OR

"Okuuuuurt! This book be flexin' on the 'gram like aye. It's so schmoney. Pop a rubber band and buy it—eeooowww!

—*Cardi B*, Grammy-dominating recording artist

CONTENTS

INTRO-DUC-TION

Hey dude, how's it going? Thanks for buying this life-changing book. We will spend your money on fun and exciting stuff, like salmon eggs, coconut butter, day care, college tuition, or a 7-day, 6-night cruise to the Hawaiian islands with an ocean view cabin. Inside (the book, not the ocean view cabin), you will get your money's worth with absolutely delicious snacks and meals that are aligned with a nutritious, well-designed ketogenic diet.

This book is guaranteed to make keto-style eating easy, fun, and time efficient. This is super important, because there are plenty of fantastic keto cookbooks out there, but the recipes often seem too complex and intimidating for even our (possibly) lazy asses to make. In this cookbook for Cool Dudes, we want you to land on a recipe page, marvel at the stunning photo, and commit on the spot to making that recipe. Since we are also very athletic, knowledgeable, and hilarious, the book will be an enjoyable read. You have written permission to repurpose our jokes and swagger to become more popular in daily life.

Making Sure This Book Is for You

If we had hired highly paid marketing consultants, they would have suggested that we carefully identify our "target market avatar"—our prototypical reader. See if this Cool Dude avatar sounds a whole lot like you:

1. Extremely good looking, clever, and creative, with a magnetic, inspiring personality.

2. Concurrently, extremely chill, self-effacing, sensitive, kind, empathetic, and totally over yourself.

3. Exceptionally competent in the conference room, classroom, boardroom, gym, athletic field, flea market, and bedroom.

4. Extremely high IQ, emotional intelligence, and street smarts.

5. Biomarkers: Serum and free testosterone at 95th percentile or above. Progressive sperm motility at 72 percent or higher, and total sperm count at 400 million or higher.

6. Highly refined sense of humor, able to regale both large and small groups at parties. But also a good listener and never hogging the spotlight, especially if it's someone else's birthday.

7. Very productive and time-efficient. Don't have time to waste on elaborate meal preparations, but too important to waste life eating processed junk food.

8. Totally not into pandering displays of any of the above. On the surface, a seemingly ordinary, fun-loving dude.

9. Not a muppet, nor hanging around muppets.*

WHAT'S A MUPPET?

*Muppet is a derogatory term appropriated by Australian Cool Dude, life coach, and elite amateur triathlete Andre Obradovic. It describes someone who just goes along with the pack in life, content to be mediocre (or even a jerk at times) instead of striving for peak performance. There are parking lot muppets (blocking traffic waiting for a close spot, instead of just f—ing walking from a distant spot); elevator muppets (they should sprint up the stairs, like Cool Dudes); husband muppets (they hear their wives talking, but don't really listen); boyfriend muppets ("Oops, I totally spaced on your birthday, sorry babe."); workplace muppets—who say "try," "sorry," and "hindsight" all the time (e.g., "In *hindsight*, I should have finished the presentation before the meeting; *sorry* about that. I'll *try* harder next time."); and of course food muppets who say, "Hey, everything in moderation, right? Might as well enjoy life, right?" and then they eat Ben & Jerry's every night while being a husband muppet. Bottom line from Andre is this: "Don't be a fucking muppet, mate."

Andre says:
"Don't be a f—ing muppet, mate!"

Are you feelin' your Cool Dude avatar right now? Thought so! Alas, please don't feel bad if you only relate to, say, five or six out of the nine bullets. As Brad's wife Mia Moore likes to say en Español, "No es un concurso"—it's not a competition here. We are just trying to agree that because you bought this book, we are on the same page, looking for many of the same pleasures and optimizations to create maximum enjoyment and happiness in life.

Going Keto the Right Way, Instead of the Muppet Way

The main purpose and benefit of the ketogenic diet is to help you escape carbohydrate dependency and build what Cool Dudes call *metabolic flexibility*. Metabolic flexibility means you are able to burn a variety of fuel sources to meet your body's needs at all times, especially stored body fat. In contrast, today's grain-based, high-carbohydrate, high insulin-producing SAD diet shuts off ketone production, inhibits fat burning, and instead makes you dependent a constant supply of dietary carbs as your main source of energy. Following an ancestral-style keto-friendly diet helps you become well adapted to burn stored body fat and manufacture ketones when you need them.

Ketones are known as the "fourth fuel"—energy-rich (five calories per gram) by-products of fat metabolism in the liver that are generated when blood glucose, blood insulin, and liver glycogen levels are low. When you are fasting or limiting carb intake to 50 grams per day or less, ketones provide an excellent fuel source for your ravenous brain, which is otherwise almost entirely dependent upon glucose. Indeed, the brain accounts for some 20 percent of your daily energy caloric expenditure, despite being only two percent of your bodyweight (2.7 percent in the case of the authors). When you build metabolic flexibility, you can skip meals without experiencing a decline in cognitive or physical function and even perform magnificent athletic feats fueled by stored fat, internally manufactured ketones, and the muscle glycogen that you are now excellent at preserving because you stopped eating garbage and overproducing insulin all day long.

> *The main purpose of keto is to build metabolic flexibility—the ability to burn a variety of fuel sources, especially stored body fat*

Ditching carb dependency and becoming fat- and keto-adapted honors your genetic capacity for health and longevity. Evidence increasingly suggests that ketones were a critical human fuel source during the 2.5 million years of our hunter-gatherer existence. Our primal ancestors ate vastly fewer carbohydrates than civilized humans, since

Slurpees® weren't yet widely available or affordable. Our ancestors routinely missed meals or strings of meals, yet still had to perform at their physical and cognitive peak to survive and thrive. It has only been since the advent of agriculture and civilization around 10,000 years ago that humans have transitioned over to a grain-based diet, and it has come at great expense to our health. The health destruction has spun out of control over the past century with the advent of industrialized food processing, especially the boat loads of processed sugar that destroy our fat burning capabilities and the sinister seed oils that cause an instant disturbance in healthy cardiovascular function.

MAKE A COOL DUDE CAMPFIRE, NOT A MUPPET CAMPFIRE

When you consume carbohydrates, they are quickly converted into glucose so you get instant energy—the familiar sugar high. Unfortunately, glucose burning generates inflammation and free radicals, because glucose can be burned directly in the cell without the use of oxygen. Carbs can be considered a dirty-burning fuel; more so with sugar than starches, but even complex carbs are eventually converted into glucose and either burned or transported out of the bloodstream by insulin and stored as triglycerides (fat). Fatty acids and ketones require oxygen to burn, so you enjoy the protective benefits of *mitochondria*. These energy-rich power plants inside each cell help you burn fuel more cleanly, without inflammation or oxidative stress (free radicals).

Carbohydrate dependency is like making a lazy muppet campfire: You burn twigs and wadded up newspaper quickly, making a lot of smoke. You need to constantly refuel (eat high-carb meals and snacks) because your chronically excessive insulin production makes stored fat inaccessible. In contrast, stored body fat and internally manufactured ketones are like the big logs in a Cool Dude campfire. Heat them up carefully (build metabolic flexibility through healthy eating, exercise, sleep, and lifestyle habits) and they keep you warm for hours with minimal smoke, and no need for wadded up newspapers.

As you may have heard, achieving nutritional ketosis entails limiting your total dietary carbohydrate intake to 50 grams or less per day. Why? This forces your liver to produce ketones to provide the brain with necessary energy in the absence of dietary carbohydrates. If carbs are available, your body won't go through the elaborate and delicate process of making ketones. However, ketones are a far more efficient and clean energy source for the brain than quick-burning glucose. Reducing carbs to 50 grams per day or below still allows for abundant vegetable intake, along with incidental carbs found in foods like nuts and nut butters, coconut milk, and dark chocolate. But that's about it. During focused periods of keto, we recommend that you limit or avoid even nutritious carbs like fruit and sweet potatoes—save those for the periods you return to eating a general low-carb, ancestral diet. But for now, going keto—kicking your body into producing and using ketones for its main energy source—necessitates greatly reducing all carbs, in addition to zero tolerance for grains, sugars, and sweetened beverages.

The Keto Reset Diet details a methodical step-by-step approach where you leverage success in each phase without suffering. For best results, we recommend that you read or listen to the book, but here is a quick Cool Dudes summary of how to go keto the right way:

Step 1: 21-Day Metabolism Reset: Ditch grains, sugars, and industrial seed oils, and replace them with your choice of nutrient-dense, ancestral foods: meat, fish, fowl, eggs, vegetables, fruits, nuts and seeds, and of course certain nutritious modern foods like high-fat dairy products and high-cacao-percentage dark chocolate. There is no concern with restricting carbs just yet, because first you have to build a proper fat burning foundation in order to obtain the desired benefits of keto.

The big three most offensive foods, grains, sugars, and industrial oils, are ubiquitous in today's food supply, and even health-conscious eaters can unknowingly ingest a bunch of this junk. For example, the Starbucks mobile ordering app has default ingredient settings for their iced teas and lemonades that include between three and seven pumps of liquid cane sugar depending on size (talli, venti, tenti, trenti, or muppeti). If you don't want your drink tainted accordingly, you must hit the minus button repeatedly to deviate from the default! Bestselling natural medicine author Dr. Andrew Weil states that 20 percent of all calories in the modern diet come from soybean oil alone. *Deep Nutrition* author Dr. Cate Shanahan cites an estimate that 40 percent of all calories consumed in restaurant meals come from industrial seed oils because they cook meals in cheap oil to save a few bucks.

Here is a quick overview of the foods and food categories to eliminate due to the presence of grains, sugars, and/or industrial oils:

Sugars and sweetened beverages: Candies, desserts, baked goods (donuts, cookies, etc.), frozen treats (ice cream, popsicles), and all sweeteners (details shortly); designer coffees (mochas, blended ice coffees, etc.), energy drinks (Red Bull, Rock Star, Muppet Fool, Monster, etc.), sweetened teas (Arizona, Nevada, Nantucket Nectar, Snapple, etc.), fruit juices, lemonade, soft drinks, sweetened non-dairy milks, sports performance drinks (Gatorade, etc.), and sweetened cocktails (margarita, daiquiri).

Grain foods: Cereal, corn, pasta, rice, and wheat; bread and flour products (baguettes, crackers, croissants, muffins, pizza, pretzels, etc.); breakfast foods (Cream of Wheat®, dried cereal, French toast, granola, grits, oatmeal, pancakes, waffles); chips (corn, potato, tortilla); cooking grains (amaranth, barley, bulgur, couscous, millet, rye); and puffed snacks (Cheetos®, Goldfish®, Lil' Muppets®, Pirate's Booty®, popcorn, rice cakes).

Industrial seed oils: Bottled high polyunsaturated oils (canola, cottonseed, corn, soybean, safflower, sunflower, etc.); buttery spreads and sprays (Smart Balance®, Promise®); margarine and vegetable shortening; salad dressings and other condiments; packaged, frozen, and baked goods; deep-fried fast food; most cooked restaurant meals (request meals cooked in butter, not oil).

DON'T FORGET TO DITCH THESE MUPPET FOODS, TOO:

Nutrient-deficient processed foods: Low or non-fat dairy products, high-carbohydrate energy bars and grain-based snacks (granola bars, energy bars), chemical-laden frozen meals.

Low quality keto-approved foods: Pre-packaged meat products, smoked/cured/nitrate-treated meats (bologna, ham, hot dogs, gas station jerky, pepperoni, salami, sausage); meat from Concentrated Animal Feeding Operations (CAFO); conventional eggs (choose pastured or at least organic); conventional produce transported from distant origins and out of season; nuts, seeds, and nut butters processed with offensive oils or sugary coatings.

During the initial 21-Day Reset, you will also focus on complementary lifestyle practices that can make or break your keto efforts. This includes:

- A sensible exercise program of frequent everyday movement

- Comfortably paced aerobic workouts

- Brief, intense strength training and sprinting sessions

- Sleeping instead of watching YouTube or Netflix

Your movement, exercise, sleep, and stress management habits will make or break the success of your keto efforts. If you are inactive, overtraining, under-sleeping, or living a high-stress muppet lifestyle, these stressful behaviors promote carbohydrate dependency. As you ditch the wrong foods and eat the right foods, get your exercise program dialed in and minimize artificial light and digital stimulation after dark. Implement calming bedtime rituals (warm bath, reading by headlamp, etc.); sleep in a calming, uncluttered, cool, and completely dark environment; and awaken near sunrise to initiate a movement routine. You will also implement healthy stress management techniques, such as getting your pathetic tech addiction under control.

MUPPET DISTRACTIBILITY

Did you know the average person reaches for their phone 150 times per day? Can you believe the typical office worker interfaces with 37 different screens each hour, spending an average of only three minutes on a task before becoming distracted? Do you think Cool Dudes could write this book with that kind of distractibility happening? No, we would be muppets instead, wishing we wrote a book for Cool Dudes.

Sorry, what were we talking about again? Oh yeah, overly stressful workout patterns, insufficient sleep, and hectic daily routines that compromise fat burning and promote carbohydrate dependency. This happens particularly at night, when your Netflix® binge-watching suppresses melatonin, spikes the prominent stress hormone cortisol, spikes the prominent hunger hormone ghrelin, and dysregulates the prominent satiety and fat storage hormone leptin. Know this: stress drives carb dependency, drives fat storage, drives accelerated aging, drives Miss Daisy crazy. Changing lanes to burn fat and ketones instead puts you in the driver's seat to health, peak physical and cognitive performance, and lifelong maintenance of ideal body composition.

It's important to realize that you're not an undisciplined loser for occasionally binging on Cocoa Puffs® at 11 p.m. These binges are actually driven by hormone imbalances that compromise healthy metabolic function. It's more accurate to say that you're an undisciplined loser for watching Netflix late at night in the first place. When you clean up your act and start burning fat and ketones instead of sugar, you will begin to experience stable energy, mood, appetite, and cognitive function all day long. Those working from a really lousy starting point may want to make this a 42- (instead of 21-) Day Reset. Take your time and proceed to the next level of metabolic flexibility when you are ready.

Step 2: Fine-tuning period: After completing the 21- or 42-Day Reset successfully, you can proceed into a fine-tuning period, centered upon a daily effort to seeing how long you can comfortably last in the morning before consuming your first calories of the day. If you can experience peak cognitive and physical function until noon without calories, then you demonstrate a respectable level of *metabolic flexibility*. If your last meal was consumed around 8 p.m. the previous evening, then you have been turbo-charging your fat burning genes for 16 hours. Many ancestral health experts believe that eating your meals in a compressed time window like this (noon to 8 p.m.) is a tremendous catalyst for not just fat reduction, but disease protection and longevity.

THE FAST-ING JOURNEY FROM SOFT, WUSSY MUPPET BOY TO THE ULTIMATE OBJECTS OF DESIRE

Dr. Art DeVany, one of the forefathers of the ancestral health movement, author of **The New Evolution Diet**, and a highly credible source on account of still being ripped at 82 years old, says that, "We are perhaps most human when we don't eat...because we turn on genes that are geared toward stress resistance, repair, and maintenance." Fasting has been scientifically validated to deliver profound anti-inflammatory, anti-aging, and immune benefits, as well as promote the natural internal cellular detoxification called *autophagy* and the desirable programmed death of dysfunctional and pre-cancerous cells known as *apoptosis.* These processes get compromised by a high-sugar, high-stress life, accelerating the aging process and increasing your disease risk factors.

Getting competent at fasting and minimizing the wildly excessive insulin production caused by high-carbohydrate eating, can literally reverse the aging process in your body. You can lower your biological age through the greatest anti-aging strategy ever discovered—fasting and becoming more calorically efficient in general (eating an optimally minimal amount of calories and producing an optimally minimal amount of insulin to survive and thrive). Your biological age is based on your functional fitness and metabolic health standard for other's your age, and is obviously younger, the same, or older than your chronological age. For example, the Cooper Institute in Dallas, TX cites performance standards in the one-mile run at age 50 as an outstanding predictor of longevity. If you can run the mile in under eight minutes (a brisk jog) at age 50, you have a lower biological age than your peers and excellent longevity prospects. If you can't break 12 minutes, your longevity prospects decline dramatically. If you can't even walk a quarter-mile in six-minutes (muppet pace), your chances of dying in five years are 300 times greater than someone with a basic level of fitness such as a 12-minute mile performance

Brad's mile time was four minutes (while carrying golf club)

Remember, there is no faking or suffering allowed when you are pursuing metabolic flexibility. If you get hungry, it's time to eat. If it happens to be at 10 a.m. one day, so be it. Recognize that you are unwinding decades of carbohydrate dependency, so the process of fat- and keto-adaptation may take some time. Keep trying, and know that escaping carbohydrate dependency gets easier over time. Pay particular attention to avoiding the refined grains and sugars that spike blood sugar, prompt an insulin release, and make it difficult to access and burn stored body fat. Because humans are genetically hardwired to prefer fat, you will likely feel great almost immediately when you ditch refined carbs and oils from your diet. When you get into the rhythm of morning fasting, or otherwise skipping lunch or dinner if more convenient, then you are ready for a successful foray into nutritional ketosis in the near future. Over time, you will likely default into a pattern of eating only one to two proper sit down meals a day, because you simply won't need so many external calories to function well. By the way, slamming a high-fat coffee in the morning does not count as "fasting." Sorry, look up fasting in the dictionary if you don't believe us.

Step 3: Go keto for six weeks: After you complete the 21-Day Metabolism Reset and feel pretty decent even after skipping breakfast, *The Keto Reset Diet* presents a midterm exam to assess whether you are ready to commence a proper keto effort. Once you pass the midterm exam—a list of subjective questions to help determine how well you are maintaining energy and focus without regular doses of carbs—you are ready to take the final step of a dedicated period of ketogenic eating for a minimum of six weeks.

After six weeks, you can relax your intense devotion to keto macronutrient guidelines if you like and celebrate your success with some sweet potatoes slathered in butter. Some people elect to eat in a ketogenic pattern indefinitely, while others choose to exist in what Mark Sisson calls the "keto zone," where carb intake might exceed keto guidelines on certain days or weeks, but the individual eliminates processed carbs, eats keto friendly meals, and emphasizes fasting and eating in a compressed time window. Either way, you can finally enjoy the benefits of a metabolically flexible, fat-adapted lifestyle. Becoming fat- and keto-adapted is like breaking free from carb prison. This is especially relevant to large segments of the population who struggle for years with assorted forms of disordered eating and failed weight loss efforts.

AVOID THE QUICK FIX APPROACH

A progressive, multi-stage approach to keto is necessary for success, because going keto in a quick fix or extreme manner will backfire on you. A sudden or extreme restriction of dietary carbohydrates before you are metabolically flexible will kick you into the dreaded chronic fight-or-flight mode. Your body will manufacture the necessary glucose for your glucose-addicted brain via a process known as *gluconeogenesis*—the converting of amino acids, particularly lean muscle tissue, into glucose. This is a fundamental element of the stress response, and is why you can stay wired for hours or days at a time without food when you are under intense deadline pressure or experiencing a crisis in your personal life.

Don't be a muppet and plunge blindly into keto without doing the proper preparation. Follow the steps, and remember that the 21-Day Reset is not just about reducing your carbohydrate intake, but also the lifestyle variables of proper exercise, sleep, and stress management. Complete the fine-tuning period so that you can gradually extend the boundaries of your metabolic flexibility, and don't start keto until you're fully ready. When it's time for your six-week journey, be sure to choose an appropriate time, when life stress is minimal and enthusiasm and resolve are high. In the first three weeks of keto, it is extremely important to minimize down your overall energy output during workouts and daily life in general. If you try to maintain your normal workout patterns without your usual carb intake, your muscles and brain will be in competition for the precious alternative fuel source of ketones. This means you'll feel sluggish in your workouts and suffer from the afternoon blues at work.

Regarding your meal choices, Brian dispensed the following sage advice during his interview on Brad's exceptionally well produced, award-winning, highly acclaimed, *Get Over Yourself* podcast: "If you are having trouble adjusting to a keto-style eating pattern, just pick some of your favorite meals and eat them over and over so you can build some momentum." This also helps you nail your macronutrient goals without having to constantly make calculations. Honor the lifestyle practices that support keto, particularly good sleep habits and minimizing total workout energy expenditure during the transition from glucose burning to fat and ketones.

Keto Macronutrient Guidelines

Instead of stuffing your face with fat during your keto efforts, implement the following macronutrient intake strategy from keto legend Luis Villasenor at Ketogains.com. Luis, known across the globe by his Internet persona "Darth Luiggi," has been in strict keto for 18 years and counting, while maintaining an extreme athletic training regimen for competitive powerlifting and bodybuilding. He's wicked smart, he's jacked AF, and he doesn't mess around. He has helped thousands of people lose weight and keep it off with a focused, no-nonsense approach. Here are Luis's brilliant macronutrient recommendations:

Luis Villasenor

Protein is a Target: The consensus among health experts, including keto leaders like Villasenor, is to obtain an average of 0.7 grams per pound of lean body mass (1.54 grams per kilo) per day. This is pretty easy to achieve if you eat a sensible diet (i.e., you're not following some freaky low protein regimen you found on the Internet). Unlike carbs, where you must observe a strict daily limit to facilitate ketone production, you can meet your protein averages over a week or a month time frame. Your body is good at compensating if you fall short or exceed protein targets on certain days.

Meeting your protein target is your primary dietary objective, but it's super easy. Don't worry about underconsuming protein, because if you happen to fall into this extremely rare pattern, you'll feel like crap, become emaciated, and experience intense cravings for high-protein foods. It's just not going to happen without you being a total doofus. Regarding overconsuming protein, the conventional thinking for years has been that too much protein can stress the liver and kidneys and overstimulate growth factors in the bloodstream like mTOR and IGF-1. This can lead to accelerated aging and increased cancer risk. Today, many experts are backing off on these dire warnings, particularly if you are healthy and athletic. Furthermore, if you eat in a low-carb pattern, ingested protein can help restock glycogen via gluconeogenesis. However, a high-protein eating pattern will compromise ketone production in the liver, so your initial foray into keto is best achieved with moderate protein intake.

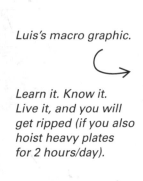

Luis's macro graphic.

Learn it. Know it. Live it, and you will get ripped (if you also hoist heavy plates for 2 hours/day).

Carbs are a *Limit*: Strive to consume 50 grams per day or less to promote ketone production in the liver, with no exceptions or "cheat days." Ketosis is a very delicate state that is immediately suspended when you consume even a moderate amount of carbs, such as a quick orange juice in the morning, or a scoop of marble slab ice cream after a surf session in San Diego. Studies from pioneering keto researchers Dr. Stephen Phinney and Dr. Jeff Volek reveal that it can take several days for a keto novice to return to nutritional ketosis after a single carbohydrate binge.

You may be familiar with the concept of net carbs, where the grams of fiber in a certain food are subtracted from total carbohydrate grams to generate a net figure. Dudes like to make things simple and count gross carbohydrate intake toward your 50-gram limit.

Here is an important caveat per Villasenor: don't worry about the carb contribution from avocados or leafy green vegetables. The fat in the avocado and the high fiber and water content of leafy greens make them inconsequential to efforts to restrict insulin production and promote ketone production. So call it 50 grams per day without counting avocadoes or leafy greens.

Another caveat: the 50 gram recommendation assumes you are quite physically active, with several hours of low-level movement each week (walking or doing mild cardio sessions) and regular high intensity resistance and/or sprint workouts. If you are a slug who rides the subway, works at a desk, and watches Fortnight experts streaming their live competitions for hours, you must stick to a limit of 20 grams. Actually, if you are leading a sedentary lifestyle, you should just get your ass moving more in daily life instead of worrying about being a Cool Keto Dude. Seriously, stop reading and go take a walk right now.

Fat is a *Lever*: The goal of your fat intake is to obtain full dietary satisfaction each day. You eat whatever amount of fat you need to feel satiated and happy. When you first wean off your lifelong consumption of comfort foods, you have permission to hit the fat liberally. The biggest goal of keto is to enjoy the process and avoid backslides, so if you need to reach for a handful of macadamia nuts every couple hours instead of reaching for a disgusting, synthetic, high-sugar energy bar or Soylent® drink, enjoy the nuts and other nutritious high-fat snacks with full attention and appreciation. As you become more fat- and keto-adapted, you will burn body fat so well you won't have to stuff your face with dietary fat.

Summary
Protein: 0.7 grams per pound (1.54 grams per kilo) of lean body mass on average per day
Carbs: 50 grams of gross carb intake (don't count avocados or leafy greens) per day
Fat: Lever to achieve dietary satiety and happiness each day.

Please fully appreciate the concept of fat as a lever instead of something to stuff in your face each day to make a perfect keto macronutrient pie chart. If you want to drop excess body fat, you will minimize dietary fat intake and make up the difference by burning stored body fat. In this scenario, your carb and protein percentages might rise above the keto boilerplate, meaning you get ripped while keto enthusiasts stuffing their face with fat get frustrated.

The Cool Dudes Keto Strategy

Brian has maintained a strict devotion to keto since April of 2016 and has only become smarter, fitter, more ripped, more popular, and more fertile—witness his daughters born in 2017 and 2019. Contrary to flawed notions of keto held by many naysayers who claim keto does not work for high-intensity athletes, Brian pairs keto with explosive powerlifting sessions in the gym with great success, fast recovery, and no ill effects. Brian reports that it's no trouble or hassle to stay in keto, because he implements an effective strategy that does not require will power or generate decision fatigue:

"I only eat keto-aligned foods and meals, so I don't even consider other options. When you build momentum by eating repeating meals, you can then get creative and try stuff from this book or the @WholeDoods Instagram page. It doesn't have to be a complex approach where you get stressed about always finding new meals. For many people, if you open yourself to other options and temptations, it becomes a slippery slope where you can easily fall off-track, get discouraged, and bail on keto entirely. You have to make keto convenient and enjoyable, and find foods and meals that you really love and want to have more than any other non-keto option."

Brad follows a more intuitive and varied eating strategy. Generally, he practices extended morning fasting and eating keto-aligned meals. He also engages in experiments to eat in a wider time window, or consume more carbohydrates than keto guidelines entail. Brad's motivations:

"The main reason for my varied approach is laziness; I am too busy with more pressing endeavors like Speedgolf to bother with tracking macros, measuring blood ketones, or stressing about an overly-regimented diet. I am quite certain that I operate in the keto zone, where my daily carb intake might range from 20 grams on a day of fasting and/or keto-aligned meals, to occasional days of 100 or 150 grams of carbs.

On days that I exceed keto, I am not hitting Starbucks caramel Frappuccinos, Ben & Jerry's nasty industrial oil-laden offerings (seriously, check their labels), nor factory-ing in any mass-produced cheesecake. Rather, I might enjoy some sweet potato fries drowned in butter and a tiny dusting of powdered sugar, per my buddy Gordon Ramsay. (Actually, I don't know him, but I know the dusted fries served in his Las Vegas restaurant are awesome.) In the hours after a rare long mountain bike ride, I might inhale a bowl of heavily buttered popcorn or large quantities of 85–90 percent dark chocolate.

Almost always, my days of increased carbohydrate intake align with ambitious workouts that I am striving to perform and recover from at the advanced age of 54. This targeted carb intake may be an effective performance and recovery strategy, or it may not matter much. After a great devotion to a low-carb ancestral-style eating pattern for a decade now, I feel like I can get away with a variety of eating strategies, from extended daily fasts to epic dark chocolate and popcorn binges, without adverse effects. With diet, the main objective is to ditch the toxic modern foods of refined grains, sugars, and industrial seed oils, emphasize colorful, nutrient-dense foods, and enjoy eating as one of the great pleasures of life."

While these stories from Brian and Brad are extremely captivating and awe-inspiring, the optimal approach to keto will vary significantly among individuals, based on your current state of metabolic health and the nature of your fitness and peak performance goals. The best approach is to complete the entire Keto Reset journey as advertised, then test out an assortment of long-term strategies. Then evaluate, modify, re-test, and repeat going forward. Even when you discover what works best for you, realize that you will likely want to modify things now and then in order to continually strive for best results.

A few foundational guidelines must be respected: First, keto should be attempted only when you are relatively healthy. If you are battling gut dysfunction, autoimmune conditions, or adrenal or thyroid dysfunction, you may want to focus on eating wholesome, nutrient-dense foods and not worry about counting macros or significantly cutting carbs until you heal your conditions and exhibit excellent general health. Second, if you are struggling to reduce excess body fat or have disease risk factors in your bloodwork, keto may be more warranted, and deliver more profound benefits, than for someone with optimal body fat and no disease risk factors. It's certain that the most reliable and straightforward way to reduce excess body fat is to lower carb intake, minimize insulin production, and turbocharge fat burning. For lean, athletic types looking for a peak performance edge, consuming a higher volume of nutrient-dense foods, including carbs to the extent that you exceed keto limits, might deliver similar results to a strict ketogenic strategy.

THE COMPELLING CARNIVORE DIET

While the idea of a carnivore diet initially raised alarm bells among both mainstream and progressive health experts, a nose-to-tail carnivore eating strategy that omits all plant foods—not just grains, but vegetables, nuts, seeds, and fruits, too—is gaining increasing scientific validity and phenomenal user success stories. Why is carnivore working and its popularity exploding? Crazy as it sounds, many of us may be mildly or significantly reactive to the **anti-nutrients** contained in assorted plant foods, even super healthy stuff like leafy greens and cruciferous veggies. It's well known that plants release defensive compounds such as **lectins** (gluten is an example of a lectin) and **phytates** to ward off garden pests, and that these agents can trigger an inflammatory and/or autoimmune response in sensitive individuals. Often, this plant reactivity is sub-clinical, stimulating low-grade inflammation or compromising the integrity of your gut lining without any noticeable

symptoms. It's a disturbing prospect to think about spending decades faithfully emphasizing so-called superfoods like kale, broccoli, onions, walnuts, hummus, and almond butter, that might be unknowingly compromising your health.

Eating only animal foods, at least for a short-term dietary restriction experiment, has produced some amazing healing stories. Leading carnivore promoter Dr. Paul Saladino (Instagram @PaulSaladinoMD) is a psychiatrist who has had outstanding results treating anxiety, depression, and assorted other mental health conditions with a carnivore dietary intervention. Carnivore enthusiast Amber O'Hearn claims to have successfully treated bipolar disorder with carnivore. Mikhaila Peterson, daughter of Dr. Jordan Peterson (Canadian psychologist, author of *12 Rules for Life*, and modern philosopher/thought leader) experienced near-miracle healing from extreme lifelong autoimmune, chronic fatigue, and depressive disorders with the carnivore diet. She went from autoimmunity so severe that resulted in hip and ankle replacements in her teens and twenties, to vibrant health in a short time. Carnivore expert Dr. Shawn Baker (Instagram @ShawnBaker1967) has broken world indoor rowing records in his 50s—powered by meat! Check out meatheals.com for tons of stunning success stories and intriguing commentary.

Since carnivore is highly satiating and nutrient dense, enthusiasts can drop excess fat without the usual hassle of extreme caloric restriction and exhaustive workouts. Carnivore advocates make a compelling case that we can obtain virtually all the nutrition we need without plants, and arguably with vastly superior nutrient density to a plant-heavy diet. Plenty of emerging science and user experiences, including favorable blood test results, easily refute the reactionary speculation that you will keel over from eating salmon, sardines, eggs, steak, and bone broth.

Brian and Brad became captivated by the burgeoning movement in 2019, and have experimented with carnivore in their quest to stay in vibrational alignment with the aforementioned avatar. In general, carnivore closely resembles keto because it is free from grains, sugars, and industrial seed oils, very low in carbs, and high in nutrient-dense animal foods. There are a couple key distinctions between carnivore and keto: First is the absence of plant foods in carnivore: no vegetables, fruits, nuts, seeds, or grains. Second, with the emphasis on nose-to-tail meats, eggs, and fish, and lack of carbs from plants, carnivore eating will result in higher protein intake than the keto template. In most cases, carnivore comes out as high protein, medium-to-high fat, and nearly zero carbs. While high-protein meals can arrest ketosis, many carnivore eaters still spend plenty of time in ketosis by eating infrequently and eating little or no carbs.

While evolutionary biology confirms that humans evolved as omnivores, Dr. Saladino makes a compelling case on his *Get Over Yourself* podcast interview with Brad that plants are merely "survival foods": They have a generally inferior nutritional value to animal foods, and were perhaps only consumed as a strategy against unsuccessful hunting. Dr. Shawn Baker offered a memorable podcast comment that if a primal hunter-gatherer band—typical size of 30 individuals—were able to bring down a prehistoric wooly mammoth, they could feast on an estimated 3 million calories for months without having to gather anything!

Regarding the predictable objection of missing out on the high antioxidant and micronutrient values in colorful plants, Dr. Saladino and other carnivore advocates point out plants generate antioxidant benefits because they are **hormetic stressors**—our bodies generate an antioxidant response to address the ingestion of a plant antigen. The benefits of antioxidants are potentially negated by our powerful internal antioxidant production mechanisms. For example, when you are fasting or introducing other hormetic stressors like cold or heat exposure, you up-regulate the internal production of the super-antioxidant **glutathione** and also optimize the aforementioned autophagy. The essential argument here is that you simply don't need plants to optimize antioxidant and immune function, especially when you can engage in other forms of hormetic stressors like sprint workouts and cold plunges.

The carnivore diet that was once considered a joke for bodybuilder freaks to get cut up for contests is rapidly gaining scientific legitimacy and stunning success stories. Clearly, when you source sustainably raised nose-to-tail animal foods, pastured eggs, wild-caught salmon, and the like, you are enjoying an incredibly nutrient-dense, high-satiety diet, with little or no allergenic or reactivity concerns from foods in the animal foods category.

Considering a radical new dietary strategy that challenges your carefully honed and rigid belief system can be a valuable exercise in open-mindedness and critical thinking. It seems that many thought leaders and progressive health enthusiasts like to contin-ually test, evaluate, refine, and retest as a lifestyle strategy. Carnivore may be worth investigating further, especially if you suffer from any frustrating autoimmune or in-flammatory conditions. If you are as intrigued as we are about the carnivore diet, check out the runaway 5-star award-winning book, *Carnivore Cooking for Cross Promotion*, or rather, **Carnivore Cooking for Cool Dudes**.

Don't Forget to Emphasize Healthy Foods

Another ridiculously lame element of the keto craze is an obsession with macros to the extent that nutrient density is de-emphasized. This is the same mistake the popular Atkins Diet made back in the 1970s. People lost body fat like crazy by restricting carbs, but the narrow emphasis of the diet on restricting carbs without sufficient regard for nutrient quality was torched by critics. Despite the successful fat loss track record, Atkins eventually fell out of favor and was replaced by the Suzanne Somers Thank You ThighMaster Diet. Today, keto opponents, including highly trained medical and nutrition professionals as well as vegan freaks with handmade picket signs, lambast keto as a "dangerous" bacon and butter diet. One sign we saw recently at a rally in Portland, OR read, **"Keto is cruel to animals and greenhouse admissions. Brown rice is more nice. Peace out."**

Just kidding (about calling vegans "freaks," not about the sign; the sign was real). Much respect to the whole foods plant-based community and anyone else who has an elevated awareness and commitment to eating healthy foods. Of course, there are also high-minded vegan/vegetarian eaters who eat a lot of jelly beans washed down with carrot-ginger-beet-kale-apple juice and a tofu and lentils main course. They are likely locked in carbohydrate dependency and are potentially nutrient-deficient due to the omission of animal foods. Time to step back, step out of your dogmatic dietary camp, and examine the bigger picture objective of eating colorful, nutrient-dense foods that you actually enjoy eating. Pursuant to this goal, please study and memorize the Primal Blueprint Food Pyramid to replace the muppet USDA Food Pyramid that was tainted by manipulative corporate lobbying and flawed science.

THE PRIMAL BLUEPRINT FOOD PYRAMID

- Nutritious, satisfying, high-nutrient-value, low-insulin-stimulating foods.
- Low carbohydrate, moderate protein, ample nutritious fats.
- Flexible choices and meal habits by personal preference.
- Free of grains, sugars, and refined vegetable oils.

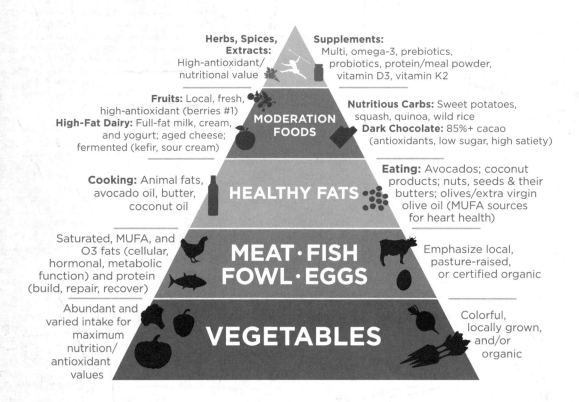

Herbs, Spices, Extracts: High-antioxidant/ nutritional value

Supplements: Multi, omega-3, prebiotics, probiotics, protein/meal powder, vitamin D3, vitamin K2

Fruits: Local, fresh, high-antioxidant (berries #1)
High-Fat Dairy: Full-fat milk, cream, and yogurt; aged cheese; fermented (kefir, sour cream)

MODERATION FOODS

Nutritious Carbs: Sweet potatoes, squash, quinoa, wild rice
Dark Chocolate: 85%+ cacao (antioxidants, low sugar, high satiety)

Cooking: Animal fats, avocado oil, butter, coconut oil

HEALTHY FATS

Eating: Avocados; coconut products; nuts, seeds & their butters; olives/extra virgin olive oil (MUFA sources for heart health)

Saturated, MUFA, and O3 fats (cellular, hormonal, metabolic function) and protein (build, repair, recover)

MEAT·FISH FOWL·EGGS

Emphasize local, pasture-raised, or certified organic

Abundant and varied intake for maximum nutrition/ antioxidant values

VEGETABLES

Colorful, locally grown, and/or organic

*Reproduced without permission because we don't need permission. Because we helped Mark Sisson formulate this stuff and road tested it with Speedgolf world records and deadlifting double bodyweight (different people).

MUPPET FOOD GUIDE PYRAMID

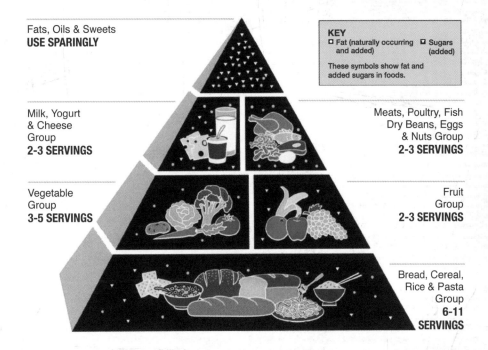

Fats, Oils & Sweets
USE SPARINGLY

KEY
▫ Fat (naturally occurring ▪ Sugars
and added) (added)

These symbols show fat and
added sugars in foods.

Milk, Yogurt
& Cheese
Group
2-3 SERVINGS

Meats, Poultry, Fish
Dry Beans, Eggs
& Nuts Group
2-3 SERVINGS

Vegetable
Group
3-5 SERVINGS

Fruit
Group
2-3 SERVINGS

Bread, Cereal,
Rice & Pasta
Group
**6-11
SERVINGS**

Most of us who have lived in America (and other nations we export trashy culture to) over the past 50 years have blindly followed government dietary recommendations without sufficient critical thinking or rigorous testing and evaluation. This qualifies us for muppet status. Don't forget the US government waited until 1965 to warn consumers about smoking, and until 1984 to mandate seatbelt use.

Time for some critical thinking: This pyramid has presided over the emergence of the fattest and least fit population in the history of humanity. Today, two-thirds of American adults are classified as overweight or obese, children have a lower life expectancy than their parents for the first time in recorded history, and Wayde van Niekerk can run a lap of a track faster than 99.9 percent of Americans can bicycle a lap. Don't be a muppet—ditch toxic nutrient-deficient foods and be a Cool Dude!

Hey Sweeties, Keep Your Distance from Cool Dudes

Many recipes in the keto world attempt to recreate the comfort foods of the grain-based, high-carbohydrate **S**tandard **A**merican **D**iet **P**eople **A**re **D**ying **F**rom **E**ating, **A**t **R**elatively **Y**oung **A**ges, **L**acking **L**ongevity (SAD PAD FEAR Y'ALL). These recipes feature keto-approved substitute ingredients like almond flour or coconut flour instead of wheat flour, and high-intensity natural sweeteners instead of sugar or other high-carb sweeteners. While modifying recipes with healthier, lower-carbohydrate ingredients is certainly a positive endeavor, it can get a little out of hand if you're not careful. If you are gleefully eating keto stevia almond flour waffles, monk fruit muffins, and keto cheesecakes all day, you may be missing the bigger picture. One of the main objectives of keto is to de-habituate away from traditions like snacking and desserts and hone the ability to access and burn stored body fat for energy.

When you succeed with detoxing and de-habituating away from sugar and the energy roller coaster of the high-carb diet, you will be amazed to discover that many of your previous food favorites (like Cheesecake produced at a Factory near you), will become disturbingly sweet and unsatisfying. With sweeteners and other substitute ingredients, use them sparingly, putting them in the "treat" category. When it comes to sweeteners, realize that coconut sugar, beet sugar, brown rice syrup, agave, organic maple syrup, and any other sweeteners touted as cleaner and healthier than nasty ol' white sugar have, calorie for calorie, a very similar effect on your body as straight sugar. In fact, when you ingest any form of carbohydrate, your body quickly converts most of it to glucose. For example, rice cakes have glycemic index value of 82, among the highest of any food (with pure glucose calibrating the scale at 100). In the context of trying to minimize insulin production and drop excess body fat, a 300-calorie serving of brown rice and lentil soup is no different than a 300-calorie serving of Skittles and root beer.

Enter the mega popularity of high-intensity natural sweeteners—stuff that has little or no calories but can be 200 times sweeter than sugar. Hence, you can use tiny amounts of these agents to sweeten large recipes without adversely impact your daily carbohydrate count. Some popular examples include stevia, monk fruit extract, erythritol, xylitol, oligosaccharides, or the branded product Swerve (made with erythritol and oligosaccharides). Erythritol and xylitol are indigestible sugar alcohols. Oligosaccharides are another form of indigestible carbohydrates that provide sweetness without the calories. Swerve is made with both erythritol and oligosaccharides. These agents are classified as high-FODMAP foods—short chain carbohydrates that pass through your intestines undigested and become fermented by the bacteria in your colon. A fair number of people complain of digestive distress from FODMAP ingestion—gas, bloating, cramping, diarrhea, and irritable bowel syndrome (IBS).

Stevia is 30 times sweeter than sugar in its natural form and up to 300 times sweeter when it's been extracted and refined (as per the consumer product you're using). Stevia gets high marks because it's natural—derived from a wild herb called *stevia rebaudiana* found in Paraguay, Brazil, and Portland, OR (Brian planted some in his back yard). Commercial stevia products are highly refined, but the FDA has given approval for the refined versions. Monk fruit also gets high marks for being natural and minimally processed, with minimal connection to digestive disturbances. It derives its sweetness from antioxidant mogrosides, and thus is believed to deliver antioxidant benefits. Some concerns with stevia and monk fruit are commercial products that are highly refined or cut with agents like dextrose, so look in quality stores or online for brands touting their purity. Some people complain that the intensity of these sweeteners can overpower the recipe.

Artificial sweeteners, known as Non-Nutritive Sweeteners (NNS), are widely regarded in progressive health circles to be bad news: Saccharin, aspartame, sucralose, acesulfame-k, and the like. These sweeteners are widely regarded by the companies that make them to be really safe and awesome to use. Studies suggest that artificial sweeteners trick the appetite center in your brain into thinking you're consuming sugar, but since you didn't really consume sugar, you may experience lingering cravings and eventually excess calorie consumption. Some evidence links artificial sweeteners to increased risk of insulin resistance, type 2 diabetes, obesity, immune dysfunction, sleep disturbances, and even stroke, heart disease, and migraine headaches. Recent research suggests that artificial sweeteners can also promote leaky gut syndrome. The connection between gut dysfunction and conditions like obesity and autoimmune conditions is strong, so it's probably wise to continue to consider artificial sweeteners as the devil, especially when much more appealing natural high-intensity sweeteners exist.

Cool Dudes Kitchen Arsenal

You will definitely need some essentials, but don't stress about having a perfectly cute kitchen with pretty copper pots hanging from racks like on the cooking shows, nor about breaking your budget with "must have" gadgets that you won't use much. Let's assume you have a functional kitchen with running water, an oven, stove, refrigerator, and basic food prep utensils. If you see an item described in a recipe that you don't have, improvise like MacGyver or order something online to be delivered within two hours by drone (okay maybe not today, but this book is designed to be relevant forever). Following is a run-down of the essentials you need to be cool, followed by a wish list that you can make people give you as gifts.

KITCHEN ESSENTIALS

Blender: You won't be royally screwed without a blender, but smoothies are a pretty awesome way to get a concentrated dose of good nutrition. We're not talking about a cheap drugstore blender, but rather a high performer like the Blendtec Total Classic Original blender (around $240 online). Cool Dudes believe that the Blendtec performs better than the higher priced Vitamix. It's a Total Classic (per Blendtec!). The Blendtec will fight valiantly to make a smoothie from even the toughest raw materials like frozen beets. Dear Blendtec, please hook us up with free blenders when this book publishes, thanks.

Cast-iron skillet: Get a huge one because it's a good arm workout to wield around, and you can make bigger portions and store them for easy reheating. Cast-iron cooking is way healthier than the chemically-treated non-stick pans that will help give you man cans and kill your libido. That said, keep in mind we're not doctors, just smarter about nutrition than the vast majority of doctors.

Cooking fats: Cook with saturated fats such as butter, animal fats (lard, bacon grease, duck fat, etc.), coconut oil, or the high monounsaturated but temperature-stable avocado oil. Extra-virgin olive oil can be used for lower heat cooking. Avoid cooking with industrial seed oils, such as canola, corn, soybean, sunflower, safflower, and so forth. These are highly toxic substances that inflict immediate damage at the cellular level when ingested. When heated, they become even more problematic to the extent that Dr. Cate Shanahan (author of *Deep Nutrition* and former director of the LA Lakers nutrition program) calls them, "free radicals in a bottle."

Glass tupperware of assorted sizes: Get a couple huge containers so you can make big batches and store. Don't use plastic Tupperware because the estrogenic compounds in the plastic will shrink your balls and raise your voice pitch. Especially when you microwave plastic, which is believed to enable the toxic molecules to leach out of the container, into your lunch, and then into your balls.

Instant Pot multiuse pressure cooker: Everyone is getting the Instant Pot, so why not you? Indeed, this unit is pretty awesome, and it's touted to replace seven common kitchen appliances (pressure cooker, Crock-Pot-style slow cooker, rice maker, egg maker, yogurt maker, steamer, and DVR recorder). It also has potential to become a counter decoration or home staging prop to loan to your realtor girlfriend. If you get a unit, discover a handful of go-to meals that you can make habitually so you get your money's worth.

Mini food processor: Great for blending nuts or vegetables. A free-standing model like the Ninja Food Chopper Express ($25 online) is fast, powerful, easy to use, and easy to clean. You can also get food processor attachments for many blenders, including Ninja blenders (but not Blendtec or Vitamix, unfortunately).

Salt: Keto enthusiasts require additional sodium and other minerals and electrolytes (potassium and magnesium especially) to account for the reduction in inflammation and fluid retention throughout the body that happens when you cut the processed crap that is high sodium and/or inflammatory (e.g., gluten) out of your diet. When you correct inflammation and fluid retention, admirers will say, "Hey, your face looks cuter!" However, you need to recalibrate your electrolyte levels by making a concerted effort to increase your intake sodium, potassium, and magnesium when you go keto.

Get a high-quality natural sea salt or mineral salt (e.g. Himalayan pink salt) instead of the more common iodized salt. Iodized salt is like junk food—it's been heavily processed, stripped of natural trace minerals, and can contain harmful chemicals for anti-clumping or colorizing. In contrast, natural, unrefined salt contains some 90 other supporting minerals and micronutrients and has a natural color of gray or pink. FYI—the only reason salt is refined and stripped of nutritional benefits is to make it look white for consumer appeal. Lame!

Spices: Strive to get organic spices, because conventional spices have been irradiated for consumer safety. This compromises the nutritional quality and generates free radicals in your spice jar. Also, believe it or not, spices can actually go rancid over time, so you should discard anything older than one year. I know, this means you might have to toss everything currently in your cupboard, but it gives you an option for a fresh start and adding key spices strategically over time. Costco's Kirkland brand offers a large size

"Organic No–Salt Seasoning" with 21 different spices. This is a great baseline product to use in nearly every recipe in this book. If you have abundant tattoos, carefully cultivated facial hair, dreads, or natural fiber-only clothing, you can obtain your spices from bulk barrels at the local co-op or independent health food market. No polo shirts, sorry.

Stirring spoons, spatulas: Use natural materials like wood and stainless steel. Throw your plastic stuff away right now before your balls shrink. Seriously, if you have any non-stick cookware or plastic utensils, you should seriously consider dumping them. If they are peeled, frayed, or otherwise imperfect, you should for sure dump them because they are likely tainting your meals with toxic chemicals.

Ziploc slider storage bags: Sliders are durable enough to pack trail mixes for travel and can hold stuff like frozen fruit or veggies for smoothies. Granted, they contain the plastic that we are so afraid of, but the convenience factor is relevant too. Try to minimize use in favor of glass, and never microwave Ziploc!

WISH LIST

Air fryer: These devices have taken the torch from the Instant Pot as the latest, greatest must-have kitchen sensation. Air fryers are essentially miniature convection ovens. They circulate hot air at high speeds to achieve a browning effect. This is the same browning you get from deep frying food like French fries, but without the health objections. Like the Instant Pot, the air fryer allows you to cook small amounts of meat or vegetables more quickly than in a regular oven. Try a salmon fillet or some Brussels sprouts and you will enjoy that nice roasted texture.

Bark recipe tools: The Stu Can't Stop Bark—dark chocolate macadamia nut bark (page 192)—is so delicious that you will be compelled to acquire the necessary items to make this for all your social gatherings:

- **Double boiler:** This is a pot stacked on top of another pot to melt chocolate or other sensitive ingredients that can't take direct heat.

- **Stainless steel scraper/chopper/chef's blade/dough scraper:** This is a sharp straight edge for cutting bark instead of cutting your finger.

Food dehydrator: This is a countertop oven-type device with numerous sliding shelves that you can stack food like meat, vegetables, herbs, nuts, and berries. Arrange your food on the shelves, and the dehydrator will slowly and gently circulate heated air through the device, creating a perfectly dried but still flavorful end product. In a few hours, you have dried plants or jerky meat that can become go-to snacks or trail food.

Change Your Life Eating Dudes Recipes!

Brian's training approach has evolved over the years. He used to be a CrossFit freak turning in long and often exhausting workouts. Realizing the high risk of overtraining, he has modified his regimen to focus on explosive lifts with plenty of recovery time between sets. This keeps the entire workout at high quality and prevents the cumulative fatigue that can lead to sugar cravings, increased injury risk, and burnout. Furthermore, he has become leaner, stronger, and more energetic in daily life to keep up with his two toddlers.

Brad credits healthy keto eating for his ever-improving Speedgolf performances. Here, Brad hits a 3-wood second shot on a difficult par-5. The ball landed in the cup on the fly.

Dude! What Are You Waiting For?

Ditching carbohydrate dependency and honing metabolic flexibility is critical to your health, but it's only part of the big picture of living a long, healthy, happy life. The dudes encourage you to adopt a comprehensive approach where you not only eat well, but exist on the planet as a kind, well-adjusted, happy, stress-balanced, creative, and energetic person. Here is a quick look at big picture health objectives to aspire to as a Cool Dude:

Move Frequently: Increasing all manner of everyday movement is now seen by experts as a more important health objective than sweating out impressive workouts in the gym or on the road. You must avoid prolonged periods of stillness that compromise fat metabolism and promote sugar cravings. JFW (Just F—ing Walk) is the centerpiece of this strategy, and you can add formal movement practices (yoga, Pilates), flexibility/mobility drills (search YouTube for "Brad Kearns Morning Routine"), and simple calisthenics like a set of deep squats in your office.

Cardio: Engage in at least a few hours a week of structured cardiovascular workouts at a comfortable aerobic heart rate, staying at or below "180 minus your age" in beats per minute. These low-stress workouts emphasize fat burning and leave you refreshed and energized afterward, instead of fatigued and depleted. 180 minus age is a surprisingly easy pace, meaning you typically have to slow your jogging or cardio machine pace to get better at burning fat.

Strength Training: Brief, intense strength training sessions boost anti-aging hormones, improve brain function, and make you generally more energetic and confident. Do sweeping, full-body functional movements like squats and deadlifts, making each set explosive and preserving excellent form. Take plenty of rest between sets to avoid cumulative fatigue that leads to burnout, sugar cravings, and performance plateaus. Thirty minutes is plenty—go hard and go home!

Sprinting: The ultimate primal workout helps turbo-charge fat burning and makes you more resilient to all other forms of exercise and general everyday stress. All you need to do is 4-10 reps lasting 10-20 seconds each. Take lengthy rest intervals so that you deliver a consistent quality of effort on every sprint. One sprint session a week is plenty to stimulate huge fitness and body composition breakthroughs.

Sleep: Getting adequate sleep must become your number-one health priority. Sleep deficiency will destroy your devoted attempts at dietary transformation and promote carb dependency, fight-or-flight excess, and declining testosterone levels. Focus on two objectives: minimizing artificial light and digital stimulation after dark, and creating a sleep sanctuary. Get your screen use out of the way early in the evening, and then wind down with relaxing activities like reading, socializing, or evening strolls. Your bedroom should be minimalist and free from clutter, cool (60-68F; 15-20C), completely dark at night, and used for sleep only. Or hey hey Borat sexy time. Niiiice!

Cold exposure: If you want to escalate your game to level 9 badass, consider a morning cold therapy regimen. You can get going by finishing your showers with two minutes of fully cold water, then escalate to a morning ice bath or chest freezer cold plunge. Every morning, Brad has programmed into habit a 4-6 minute immersion into his chest freezer (unplugged, duh…) filled with 34-38F (1-4C) water. He starts with a full immersion, then emerges to complete a sequence of 20 deep, diaphragmatic breaths cycles in the tub. He and other cold exposure proponents cite extensive research that this hormetic stressor builds mental resiliency and focus, attributes that hopefully carry over into all over forms of stress in life. By focusing on breath, you can avail a meditative experience that helps you better tolerate the cold without freaking out and launching into shallow, panting, muppet breath patterns.

Science reveals a wide assortment of cold water or cryotherapy benefits, including an awesome morning wakeup call, improved blood circulation and oxygen delivery, enhanced immune function, anti-inflammatory benefits, recovery benefits, and enhanced fat metabolism. Even a 20-second plunge into 40F (4.4C) water has been shown to boost the prominent motivation and mood-elevating hormone norepinephrine for up to an hour afterward. Vinny Van Patten, or rather Vinny van Gogh, was treated for depression in an asylum with two-hour cold baths twice a week. Search YouTube for "Brad Kearns Chest Freezer Cold Plunge" to be further regaled.

 **Quit Being a Dickhead to Your Girlfriend/Wife:** John Gray, Ph.D., the number-one bestselling selling relationship author of all-time with his *Men Are from Mars, Women Are from Venus* book series, dispensed life-changing advice during his *Get Over Yourself* podcast interview with Brad: "Males, you must not speak if you have a negative emotional charge. If you are too sensitive, emotionally needy, and demanding, it's a turn off. Instead, take some 'cave time' and engage in testosterone-boosting activities (workouts, watching sports, handyman projects). Your primary biological role is to protect your woman, most importantly from your own anger! When you say, 'I feel hurt,' this is death to a relationship. Don't talk—how many times do I have to tell you this!" Seriously, the dude said all that, and he knows his shit!

Brad and Brian encourage you to quit making excuses and start living the healthy, fit, active lifestyle that brings you energy, happiness, and longevity. *Disclaimer:* Results may vary. If you want to try to beat Brad at Speedgolf, you will have to practice running and golf for 90-120 minutes per day for 11 years. If you want to dead lift three times your bodyweight like Brian, you will have to start slowly with a basic strength training routine, then get proper coaching to safely progress with strength and prevent injury.

AND
NOW
FOR THE
RECIPES ⟩

BREAK-FAST
MEALS

Obviously, the term breakfast means to break a fast, typically with your first meal of the day after an evening's sleep. It's time to reject the conventional notion of the All-American breakfast based around carbohydrate staples consumed in the morning hours. When you wake up and stuff your face with pancakes, waffles, muffins, cereal, oatmeal, fruit juice, and other dosages of sugar, you set in motion a horrible chain of events that leads to lifelong accumulation of excess body fat.

All of us awaken in a nice fat- and ketone-burning state every morning, thanks to our overnight fast. If you stuff your talk hole with an All-American breakfast (or All-Australian breakfast if you will—yes, they have muppets Down Under who eat similarly bad morning junk), you immediately shut off fat burning and start the sugar burning roller coaster ride that lasts all day: quick energy from the sugar and beige glop, followed by an insulin release that makes you feel tired and hungry for a mid-morning snack, which gives a quick high, another insulin crash, and so on.

The Break-Fast meals in this book might seem weird, but any healthy food can be eaten any time when you are a Cool Dude. So break-fast might happen at 12 noon and it might be a couple squares of **Stu Can't Stop Bark** (page 192) or leftovers from the previous evening's entrée like **African Fish Ballz** (page 65). It could be a **Super Nutrition Green Smoothie** (page 206) at 7 a.m. before you head out for a busy day, eating nothing until a delicious evening meal. Whatever works best for you—hopefully you'll enjoy the suggestions in this section.

BACON & MUSHROOM SCRAMBLE

If you need to impress someone, just buy brie cheese. There. Done. But to really impress, make this scramble. It's the perfect combination of texture and flavor and increases your cool factor by a good 10% each time you serve it.

INGREDIENTS

6 slices of bacon

1 cup (75 g) cremini mushrooms

Sea salt & pepper

4 eggs

2 ounces (56 g) brie cheese

COOKING TIME:
20 MINS
SERVINGS:
2

WHAT TO DO

1. Fry bacon in a cast-iron skillet on medium-high heat until it is crispy and set aside, leaving the grease in the pan.

2. Slice the mushrooms and cook in the skillet, seasoning with sea salt and pepper and tossing with a metal spatula.

3. Crack the eggs directly into the skillet, season with sea salt and pepper, and begin scrambling. It's OK for the whites and yolks to cook somewhat separately; you'll appreciate the distinct flavors in your scramble when it's on your plate (and in your mouth!).

4. Serve on a plate with brie cheese, broken up on top of the scramble.

MACRONUTRIENTS PER SERVING: CALORIES: 378 FAT: 29 G CARBS: 3 G PROTEIN: 27 G

CANNED SALMON EGG BAKE

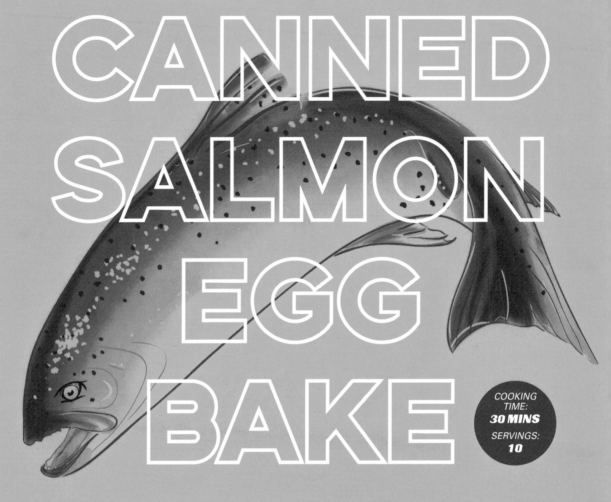

COOKING TIME: 30 MINS
SERVINGS: 10

Doesn't get much lazier than this—for both recipe and description…#I'm eating this.

INGREDIENTS

6 ounces (170 g) of canned salmon

1 egg

2 tablespoons (30 g) Primal Kitchen Avocado Oil Mayo

WHAT TO DO

1. Preheat oven to 400F (204C).

2. Open can of salmon and mix with the mayo, then spread in an even layer in a cast-iron skillet.

3. Crack an egg and let it sit on top.

4. Bake for 20-25 minutes or until the white is crispy and the yolk is still a little runny.

5. Serve with a side of pickles or sauerkraut.

MACRONUTRIENTS PER SERVING: CALORIES: 540 FAT: 43 G CARBS: 1 G PROTEIN: 45 G

BREAKFAST PATTIES

COOKING TIME:
15 MINS
SERVINGS:
8

Once you know that you can make really good tasting breakfast sausage all by yourself, you'll take all of the other risks in life that you've been putting off. That might be a stretch, but it might not. Give this a try. You'll see how easy it is to make good breakfast meat.

INGREDIENTS

1 pound (454 g) of ground pork

Sea salt and pepper

1 teaspoon (3 g) garlic powder

1 tablespoon (6 g) dried fennel seeds

WHAT TO DO

1. Gently mix ground pork, sea salt, pepper, garlic powder, and dried fennel seeds in a large mixing bowl with your hands.

2. Form into 8 patties and set aside on a plate.

3. Wash hands and heat up a skillet to medium-high.

4. Cook patties for 5 minutes per side or until it is no longer pink in color.

MACRONUTRIENTS PER SERVING: CALORIES: 152 FAT: 12 G CARBS: 1 G PROTEIN: 10 G

CORNED BEEF *BREAKFAST SKILLET*

We think that most people make a big corned beef so that they can add it to scrambles the next day, but we're biased (but willing to talk about it). In a pinch, and that's how it is for us most days, use deli pastrami and ditch the caraway seeds if it's too annoying to find them at the grocery store (hint, they're located in the spice aisle).

INGREDIENTS

6 ounces (170 g) leftover corned beef or deli pastrami

1 medium (160 g) onion

1 large (150 g) bell pepper (red and green work great)

1 tablespoon (15 g) ghee or butter

Sea salt, pepper & garlic powder

½ teaspoon (1 g) caraway seeds

WHAT TO DO

1. Chop up corned beef or pastrami, onions, and bell peppers and add to a big cast-iron skillet set to medium-high heat.

2. Add ghee or butter, sea salt, pepper, a sprinkle of garlic powder, and caraway seeds and toss with a metal spatula.

3. Continue to toss every now and then until everything has softened and browned, about 10 minutes.

4. Serve by itself or with a couple of fried eggs.

COOKING TIME:
20 MINS
SERVINGS
2

MACRONUTRIENTS PER SERVING: CALORIES: 239   FAT: 11 G   CARBS: 12 G   PROTEIN: 21 G

COWBOY
SAUSAGE GRAVY

Truthfully, real cowboys are not making this gravy, but that's only because they're too busy roping up cattle to have ordered coconut milk and almond butter on the World Wide Web. Help a cowboy out and let them know about this recipe for gravy as soon as you can, and the world will be a much better place.

INGREDIENTS

1 tablespoon (15 g) ghee or butter

1 pound (454 g) of ground pork

7 ounces (207 ml), or half of a 13.5 ounce-can (398 ml) of full fat coconut milk

1 tsp. smoked paprika

1 tsp. dried oregano

1 tsp. dried fennel seeds

Sea salt & pepper

2 tablespoons (30 g) creamy almond butter

WHAT TO DO

1. Melt a tablespoon (15 g) of ghee in a skillet set to medium heat.

2. Add ground pork, breaking up with a wooden spoon.

3. Once the pork is cooked through, add canned coconut milk (no need to drain pork grease because this is cowboy style, remember), smoked paprika, dried oregano, fennel seeds, sea salt, and pepper.

4. Stir in almond butter. Gravy will be thick and tasty.

COOKING TIME:
20 MINS
SERVINGS
4

MACRONUTRIENTS PER SERVING: CALORIES: 559   FAT: 48 G   CARBS: 5 G   PROTEIN: 24 G

CREAMY SCRAMBLED EGGS

People think you need to whisk eggs in a bowl before scrambling, but that takes time and just dirties another bowl, so simply crack them in the pan and break up with a spatula. It's actually a really brilliant way to make eggs; you'll see soon, since you're about to make this recipe. A big spoonful of mayo makes this better than plain ol' eggs.

INGREDIENTS

1 teaspoon (5 g) ghee or butter

3 eggs

Sea salt & pepper

2 tablespoons (30 g) Primal Kitchen Avocado Oil Mayo

WHAT TO DO

1. Melt a tablespoon (15 g) of ghee or butter in a skillet set to medium heat.

2. Crack eggs in the skillet and break up with a spatula.

3. Sprinkle with sea salt and pepper and scramble until cooked through.

4. Serve with mayo.

COOKING TIME:
5 MINS
SERVING:
1

MACRONUTRIENTS PER SERVING: CALORIES: 455   FAT: 43 G   CARBS: 3 G   PROTEIN: 18 G

CURRIED CAULIFLOWER EGG BAKE

Look, sometimes it's necessary to make an impressive breakfast, and this is just one way to do that. A bit unexpected for morning, but that's the whole point. You will really impress by adding some fresh herbs to this after it's out of the oven. You're welcome.

INGREDIENTS

1 16-ounce (454 g) bag of pre-cut cauliflower florets

1 tablespoon (15 g) ghee or butter

Sea salt & pepper

1 tablespoon (7 g) curry powder

4 eggs

WHAT TO DO

1. Preheat oven to 400F (204C).

2. Toss cauliflower with ghee or butter, sea salt, pepper, and about 1 tablespoon (7 g) of curry powder.

3. Bake in a skillet, uncovered, until soft, about 20 minutes, tossing after 10 minutes.

4. Crack eggs over cauliflower and bake for another 7 minutes or until egg whites are cooked through. Fancy this up with some fresh herbs as a garnish, such as parsley, cilantro, or chives.

COOKING TIME:
25 MINS
SERVINGS:
2

MACRONUTRIENTS PER SERVING: CALORIES: 278 FAT: 17 G CARBS: 16 G PROTEIN: 16 G

CURLEY BOYS'
BREAKFAST
SQUARES OR MUFFINS

Make a huge batch and then you can heat up servings for a quick morning meal on the go. But don't eat and text and drive. Don't even text and drive. Muffins are cool, but just use a baking pan if you are lazy, then cut out an appropriate serving each day. PS – The Curley boys are real brothers who used to inhale these muffins on wild outdoor global adventures—before they got real jobs, houses, and wives. Now they inhale them before a hard day's work schlepping Salomon shoes.

INGREDIENTS

1 pound (454 g) of grass-fed ground beef, lamb, or buffalo

2 cups (200 g) of chopped vegetables: onion, mushroom, pepper, kale, spinach, broccoli bits, tomatoes

12 eggs: use pasture raised, unless you are dumb and like nutritionally inferior industrial eggs

Optional: sun-dried tomatoes, feta or mozzarella cheese, bacon (previously cooked)

Spices: Real Salt or other quality natural salt, mixed spices from Costco or Trader Joe's. Or, order Cool Dudes mixed spices online (just kidding, we don't sell spices)

WHAT TO DO

1. Preheat oven to 350F (175C).

2. Sauté mixed veggies in 1 tablespoon (15 g) of butter or oil (avocado, coconut, or olive).

3. Chop up the ground meat and fry in different pan, or same pan if you are lazy.

4. Break the egg shell and drop contents into bowl. Repeat 12 times. Mix it together.

5. Mix ingredients together and pour into baking pan. If you want muffins, borrow a muffin tin from a female neighbor, friend, or family member. Spray each hole with nonstick. Fill each hole halfway with eggs, then top off with meat and veggie mixture.

6. Bake at 350F (175C) for 20–25 minutes, or until you see a little browning of top layer.

MACRONUTRIENTS PER SERVING: CALORIES: 297   FAT: 19 G   CARBS: 4 G   PROTEIN: 28 G

Curley Boys' Muffins

Conner
Curley

Tyler
Curley

DRY OATMEAL

The stovetop ancestral oatmeal preparation with the egg yolks is pretty fantastically awesome, but if you want something even quicker and easier, this preparation is the fastest breakfast or post-workout snack you can imagine. It has an interesting mix of flavors and distinct textures. It will also "stick to your bones" like grandma's oatmeal, but without the insulin spike.

INGREDIENTS

1 tablespoon (15 g) of coconut butter (puree coconut flakes if you can't find coconut butter at your local store)

2 tablespoons (30 g) of almond butter or peanut butter

2 tablespoons (30 g) of cacao nibs

2 tablespoons (12 g) of shredded coconut

⅓ cup (80 ml) of coconut milk or almond milk

WHAT TO DO

1. Smush the dry ingredients together so it has a paste consistency.

2. Add the milk and stir it up into a porridge consistency.

3. Enjoy cold. If you wanna get crazy, throw some pomegranate seeds on there.

COOKING TIME:
5 MINS
SERVING:
1

MACRONUTRIENTS PER SERVING: CALORIES: 444 FAT: 39 G CARBS: 18 G PROTEIN: 11 G

EGGCELLENT EGG BAKE

This will serve a grand gathering for brunch as easily and deliciously as anything you can possibly imagine. You know this whole book is all about making cooking quick, easy, and fun, but it's hard to top the Eggcellent Egg Bake for ease and deliciousness. You chop up a bunch of stuff, mix up some eggs, pour it into the dish, and 30 minutes later you have a colorful centerpiece meal. No offense, but this recipe blows doors on all the trendy brunch places in a hipster city near you. You'll have this whole thing completed in around 45 minutes, same as the typical Sunday wait time at the hipster spot. The next time someone says, "Epic party last night dude, let's walk down to {fill in the blank} for brunch!", just say, "Forget that, I'll just make the Eggcellent Egg Bake!"

COOKING TIME:
1 HR 5 MINS
SERVINGS:
10

INGREDIENTS

18 slices of bacon

18 eggs

3 ounces (85 g) of sliced high-quality cheese, such as raw milk

1 cup (240 ml) of organic heavy whipping cream

1 medium onion (160 g), chopped

3 cups (575 g) of broccoli, finely chopped

2 cups (300 g) red bell peppers, finely chopped

2 cups (60 g) of spinach

Salt, pepper, and mixed spices

WHAT TO DO

1. Preheat oven to 350F (175C).

2. Cook the bacon on a cookie sheet for 30 minutes or until done to perfection.

3. While the bacon is cooking, mix the chopped vegetables, eggs, cream, and spices together in a bowl.

4. Crumble the bacon and combine it with the egg mixture.

5. Pour in a 9 x 13" baking pan greased with butter and bake at 350F (175C) for 35 minutes or until a knife comes out clean and/or until the top starts browning.

5. Turn the oven off and add thin strips of cheese to the top. Allow the cheese to melt, and serve.

MACRONUTRIENTS PER SERVING: CALORIES: 331 FAT: 47 G CARBS: 6 G PROTEIN: 17 G

FRIED
BACON & CABBAGE
SCRAMBLE

Pre-shredded cabbage may be one of the best things for the keto dude. It's really easy to slice up some cabbage, but it's even easier to buy it bagged. Invest in a pair of kitchen scissors to easily slice bacon into little bite-sized fantasies and wow, you just climbed Everest!

INGREDIENTS

2 slices of bacon

1 cup (100 g) of shredded cabbage

Sea salt & pepper

2 eggs

COOKING TIME: **10 MINS**

SERVINGS: **1**

WHAT TO DO

1. Cook bacon in a skillet until crispy.

2. With the bacon still in the skillet, mince up with a pair of kitchen scissors.

3. Add a bag of shredded cabbage and toss in the bacon grease with a metal spatula, cooking until soft, about 5 minutes.

4. Season with sea salt and pepper.

5. Crack eggs over the cabbage and bacon and break up with the spatula, tossing everything together, until the eggs are cooked through.

6. Serve immediately, maybe with some avocado or a drizzle of olive oil.

MACRONUTRIENTS PER SERVING: CALORIES: 220 FAT: 16 G CARBS: 6 G PROTEIN: 18 G

DUDES COOKING KETO

Hot Summer Day
BUT
COLD KETO BREAKFAST BOWL

Some days it's too hot to cook even the quickest meal, so may we introduce to you the cold keto bowl to save the day. Better for you than cereal, best to prepare when you're out of leftovers to serve for breakfast.

INGREDIENTS

Lime juice

½ medium (75 g) avocado

Sea salt & pepper

2 soft or hard-boiled eggs

5 cherry tomatoes

WHAT TO DO

1. Mash up avocado with sea salt, pepper, and lime juice. A fork or potato masher both work well for this.

2. Serve with peeled soft or hard-boiled eggs and sliced cherry tomatoes. Amp this up with some fresh cilantro or scallion.

COOKING TIME:
5 MINS
SERVINGS:
1

MACRONUTRIENTS PER SERVING: CALORIES: 277   FAT: 21 G   CARBS: 11 G   PROTEIN: 14 G

NORI BREAKFAST BURRITO

Nori makes for a great tortilla substitute, especially when used with eggs where the moisture from them helps soften and seal the nori wrap together. We like to hide nutrient-dense Braunschweiger in ours.

INGREDIENTS

5 eggs

4 ounces (113 g) of Braunschweiger

8 sheets of nori

Tapatio/Cholula hot sauce

Optional: butter or cooking oil

WHAT TO DO

1. Cook Braunschweiger in a frying pan until browned. The sausage might have enough fat content to cook itself and the eggs in, depending on what kind you use, but if not, add some cooking oil.

2. Add the eggs and scramble.

3. On your countertop, lay out 4 nori sheets in a big square but overlapping in the middle. There should be enough eggs and sausage to make two "noritos" of 4 sheets each.

4. Pour eggs in a line down the middle and attempt to wrap like a burrito.

5. Serve with hot sauce.

COOKING TIME:
20 MINS
SERVINGS:
2

MACRONUTRIENTS PER SERVING: CALORIES: 403   FAT: 30 G   CARBS: 8 G   PROTEIN: 27 G

DUDES' FASTING BREAKFAST

DUDES' FASTING BREAKFAST

COOKING TIME:
0 MINS
SERVINGS:
1

INGREDIENTS

None

WHAT TO DO

1. Wake up and don't eat any food. While people use lame terms like "juice fast" or "brown rice fast," fasting means not consuming any calories. Instead, drink a tall glass or water, herbal tea, or black coffee when you wake up, and then see how long you can sustain peak energy, mood, and cognitive function without eating. Don't struggle or fight through authentic signals of hunger, because this may kick you into a fight-or-flight response and gluconeogenesis.

2. If you feel your stomach growlin', this is a sign of true hunger and the up-regulation of the prominent appetite-stimulating hormone *ghrelin*. As Dr. Cate Shanahan likes to say, "Ghrelin gets your stomach growlin'." Experiencing hunger is a cue to sit down for a nutritious keto-aligned meal such as an omelet. As you progress further with keto-friendly diet and lifestyle patterns, you will be able to naturally and comfortably last longer in the morning without food and feel great. If you can make it from say, an 8 p.m. dinner the previous evening until 12 noon the following day, you earn a gold star for fat- and keto-adaptation. The Dudes' Fasting Breakfast is literally one of the healthiest recipes in this entire book.

MACRONUTRIENTS PER SERVING: CALORIES: 0 FAT: 0 G CARBS: 0 G PROTEIN: 0 G

ENTRÉE MEALS

AFRICAN
FISH BALLZ

COOKING TIME:
20 MINS
SERVINGS:
4

This is another West African style recipe that Brian stole from his wife. It requires a powerful high-speed blender, so anything less than a Vitamix or Blendtec probably won't make the cut. Make sure you clean the blender very well before making your Super Nutrition Green Smoothie the next morning.

INGREDIENTS

One whole fish, with skin and bones and all

3 tablespoons (45 g) natural, unsweetened peanut butter

½ (80 g) medium onion

1 garlic clove

Salt and pepper

Avocado oil spray

Optional: 1-2 peppers (jalapeno, habanero, serrano)

WHAT TO DO

1. Cut off fish head and tail and remove the main vertebrae from the meat and skin. It's okay if a few bones get left in, since they will get smashed up by the blender.

2. Blend the fish with the peanut butter, onion, garlic salt & pepper, and optional spicy peppers. Start blender on low speed and gradually ramp up until you form a slurry.

3. Form golf ball or smaller sized balls and set aside.

4. Heat cooking pan to medium-low heat and coat with a layer of avocado oil spray to prevent sticking.

5. Add fish balls to the pan and add water so that the balls are sitting in about ½ inch of water.

6. Cover pan and let cook for about 20 minutes or until balls start to brown and caramelize on the outside.

MACRONUTRIENTS PER SERVING: CARBS: 239   FAT: 12 G   CARBS: 5 G   PROTEIN: 26 G

ANTIPASTI SALAD

Make this salad soon and you'll know all about flavor town. Don't worry about the salt in this dish, your body is craving it now that you're a bona fide Keto Dude.

INGREDIENTS

Salad

3 ounces (85 g) of salami

⅓ cup (60 g) jarred roasted red peppers

10 Kalamata olives

1 ounce (28 g) feta cheese

2 cups (150 g) butter lettuce

Vinaigrette

2 tablespoons (30 ml) olive oil

Sea salt, pepper & garlic powder

1 tablespoon (15 ml) apple cider vinegar or balsamic vinegar (or a splash of both)

WHAT TO DO

1. Chop all ingredients on a cutting board and add to a large mixing bowl.

2. Toss with olive oil, a sprinkle each of sea salt, pepper, garlic powder, and apple cider vinegar or balsamic vinegar.

3. Serve and enjoy.

COOKING TIME: **10 MINS** SERVINGS: **1**

MACRONUTRIENTS PER SERVING: CALORIES: 735 FAT: 76 G CARBS: 10 G PROTEIN: 24 G

BADASS BURGER INFUSION

COOKING TIME:
30 MINS

MAKES:
20 PATTIES

Start with some exceptionally high-quality ground meat and infuse with this creative blend to make a softer, more delicious burger. Ground buffalo is the bomb and a refreshing upgrade from the typical ground beef offerings. Visit WildIdeaBuffalo.com to learn about these amazing free-range, grass-fed, humanely harvested animals that represent one of the best choices in premium beef. Ground lamb is also awesome; choose New Zealand varieties, because all New Zealand lamb is grass-fed. Japanese style wagyu beef is also superior.

If you are using ground beef, go grass-fed or at least organic or go home. It's time to reject conventional ground beef. They are fed chemical-laden grains (that ruin their fatty acid profile) and even candy (with the wrappers still on) while fattening up like crazy for a traumatic slaughter. *Fact*: Forty million cattle are slaughtered each year in filthy slaughterhouses and packing houses. Only 60,000 buffalo are humanely harvested each year.

INGREDIENTS

4 pounds (1820 g) of ground buffalo, lamb, wagyu, or grass-fed beef

1 pound (454 g) of liver

1 medium (160 g) red onion

2 cups (250 g) of walnuts, pecans, almonds, or other nut

2 pastured eggs

3 tablespoons (21 g) of sun-dried tomatoes (make sure your brand don't got nasty industrial seed oil in the jar)

2 tablespoons (30 g) of plain full-fat yogurt

¼ cup (60 ml) fresh or bottled lemon juice

2 cups (134 g) of fresh organic kale

Spices: generous applications of mineral salt and mixed spices

Melted cheese to add onto the patties just before they're done

1 medium (150 g) avocado for topping the finished patties

WHAT TO DO

1. Wash your hands. Why do we even have to remind you? Should be obvious.

2. Use a big Cuisinart or multiple uses of small Ninja to puree all the ingredients in this exact order: whatever you want first, followed by whatever you want next, etc. till they are in there and mixed up.

3. Throw everything into large mixing bowl and shape into patties. If you find your mixture isn't forming patties easily, or if your patties don't hold their form once you start cooking them, just mince it all up in the skillet; it will still taste like the best thing, ever.

4. Melt 2 tablespoons (30 g) of butter on your huge ass heavy-duty cast-iron skillet, heated to medium-high.

5. Cook the patties on medium-high with the skillet covered. Realize these will be softer than straight ground meat. It's okay to cut into one to make sure the interior is cooked completely. Ideally you will bite into a browned, slightly crunchy exterior and a delicious soft interior which will take between 4–6 minutes per side. Cook the patties in batches since you'll be making a lot and enjoying leftovers. Serve with sliced avocado on top. Realize that with a meal this good, you never need a bun, and may never eat a chemically flavored fast food burger again.

MACRONUTRIENTS PER SERVING (w/ ½ oz of cheese):
CALORIES: 363   FAT: 22 G   CARBS: 4 G   PROTEIN: 24 G

BAKED BACON
CHICKEN BREAST

This is how you know you're cool: You can make this chicken. Whatever anyone else is saying about how to be cool, just smile and nod and when you're done affirming others, go home and make this chicken and call it another successful day.

INGREDIENTS

8 ounces (227 g) chicken breasts (boneless & skinless)

1 tablespoon (15 g) ghee

Sea salt, pepper & garlic powder

2 tablespoons (30 g) mustard (any variety, but remember, Dijon is very strong)

1 tablespoon (3 g) dried rosemary

4 slices of bacon

WHAT TO DO

1. Preheat oven to 400F (204C).

2. Place chicken breasts in a cast-iron skillet and coat with ghee or butter, mustard, and an even layer of sea salt, pepper, and garlic powder.

3. Bake in the oven for 30 minutes, flipping with a metal spatula after 15 minutes.

4. Flip once more and shove to one side of the skillet, making room to add a couple of strips of bacon.

5. Continue to bake until the bacon is done, about 15 minutes. (Cook a minute or two less if you're using very thin slices of bacon. Keep an eye on it every 5 minutes or so to keep it from burning.)

COOKING TIME: **50 MINS**

SERVINGS **2**

MACRONUTRIENTS PER SERVING: CALORIES: 322 FAT: 19 G CARBS: 3 G PROTEIN: 35 G

Berry & Beans SALAD

COOKING TIME:
10 MINS
SERVINGS:
1

Berry & Beans Salad?! We're using green beans here, folks, because we didn't forget that this is a keto cookbook and spiking insulin with legumes is simply not cool anymore! Feel free to cook these French green beans or leave them raw; both options offer a satisfying experience.

INGREDIENTS

2 tablespoons (30 g) Primal Kitchen Avocado Oil Mayo

Sea salt & pepper

½ cup (75 g) French green beans

2 medium (8 g) radish

2 cups (60 g) spinach

4 ounces (113 g) leftover chicken

¼ cup (25 g) berries (raspberries, blackberries or blueberries...even strawberries!)

WHAT TO DO

1. Add mayonnaise to a mixing bowl with a sprinkle of sea salt and pepper and mix well.

2. Chop green beans, radish, spinach, and leftover chicken.

3. Fold into the mayonnaise and serve in a bowl with a handful of berries and maybe even some chopped nuts or avocado.

MACRONUTRIENTS PER SERVING: CALORIES: 414 FAT: 28 G CARBS: 13 G PROTEIN: 33 G

BISON STUFFED PEPPERS

We kept this recipe for bison stuffed peppers pretty simple, but jazz it up and go wild by adding some dried cumin, hot sauce, or shredded cheese to the ground bison. Bake this when you've got company coming over; they won't be able to get over how cool you are.

INGREDIENTS

1 pound (454 g) of ground bison (we won't rat on you if you use beef, turkey, or chicken)

4 large (600 g) bell peppers (red, green, orange, or yellow)

Sea salt, pepper & garlic powder

1 tablespoon (7 g) smoked paprika

Fresh herbs (cilantro, parsley, or basil, or all!)

WHAT TO DO

1. Preheat oven to 400F (204C).

2. Slice the tops off of your peppers and toss out the flesh and seeds.

3. Gently toss the ground bison, sea salt, pepper, garlic powder, and smoked paprika in a large mixing bowl.

4. Mince fresh herbs and fold into the bison.

5. Fill each pepper with ground beef and arrange in a baking dish.

6. Bake until bison is cooked through and peppers are soft, about 45 minutes.

7. Impress even more by serving it with a side of cauliflower rice.

COOKING TIME:
1 HOUR
SERVINGS:
4

MACRONUTRIENTS PER SERVING: CALORIES: 305   FAT: 19 G   CARBS: 10 G   PROTEIN: 23 G

BLUEBERRY CHICKEN SALAD

Look. You gotta cook meat on keto, so when you do, make a big batch so that using it in leftovers, like this salad, is really, really easy. Blueberries scream (we exaggerate) for herbs de Provence, so enter the middle section of your grocery store, sprinkle away, and get fancy with this dish.

INGREDIENTS

4 ounces (113 g) leftover chicken

¼ cup (25 g) blueberries

2 cups (150 g) romaine, spinach or baby kale

2 tablespoons (30 ml) olive oil

Sea salt & pepper

1 teaspoon (5 g) herbs de Provence

1 tablespoon (15 ml) lemon juice

WHAT TO DO

1. Chop up some leftover chicken and toss it in a big mixing bowl with greens and a handful of blueberries.

2. Add olive oil, a sprinkle of sea salt and pepper, herbs de Provence, and lemon juice to the bowl and toss.

3. Serve and enjoy, maybe topping with a small handful of nuts or a spoonful of goat cheese.

COOKING TIME:
10 MINS
SERVINGS:
1

MACRONUTRIENTS PER SERVING: CALORIES: 437 FAT: 31 G CARBS: 10 G PROTEIN: 31 G

BOWL OF SQUASH & MEAT

There are several ways you can cook a spaghetti squash. This recipe suggests roasting it in the oven, but feel free to steam it, pressure cook it, microwave it…you're getting it now.

INGREDIENTS

1 4-pound spaghetti squash (enough to yield 5 cups or 600 g of cooked squash)

1 pound (454 g) of ground meat (beef, bison, pork, turkey, or chicken)

1 medium (160 g) yellow onion

Sea salt, pepper & garlic powder

⅓ cup (45 g) pine nuts

TIME:
1 HOUR
SERVINGS:
4

WHAT TO DO

1. Preheat oven to 400F (204C).

2. Cut spaghetti squash in half and scoop out the seeds and toss.

3. Bake on a tray until soft, about 45 minutes.

4. While the squash is baking, add ground meat to a skillet set to medium heat, breaking up with a wooden spoon.

5. Season with sea salt, pepper, and about a sprinkle of garlic powder.

6. When the squash is cooked through, remove from the oven, let cool, and scrape the flesh out with a large fork into the skillet with the ground beef.

7. Toss well and serve with pine nuts; and if you really want to impress, garnish with some fresh parsley or basil.

MACRONUTRIENTS PER SERVING: CALORIES: 361 FAT: 23 G CARBS: 14 G PROTEIN: 25 G

COOKING TIME:
45 MINS
SERVINGS:
4

Cooking with lemon slices transforms a dish with their bright and complex flavor. We like to use them as often as possible. Keep lemons stocked in your fridge and add them to roasted veggies and meats, ensuring to toss their seeds, which though tiny in size, pack an undesirable bitter flavor.

BRAISED CHICKEN WITH LEMON

INGREDIENTS

1 tablespoon (15 g) ghee or butter

1 medium (160 g) onion

1 pound (454 g) boneless & skinless chicken thighs

Sea salt & pepper

1 13.5-ounce can (398 ml) of full-fat coconut milk

1 tablespoon (7 g) dried yellow curry powder

Lemon

WHAT TO DO

1. Heat a big spoonful of ghee or butter in a skillet or Dutch oven set to medium–high heat.

2. Peel and chop an onion (yellow or white work great) and sauté until soft, about 5 minutes.

3. Add chicken thighs and sprinkle with sea salt, pepper, and garlic powder.

4. Reduce heat to a simmer and add the can of coconut milk, curry powder, and a seeded and sliced lemon and gently stir everything together.

5. Simmer until the coconut milk has thickened and the chicken is very tender, about 30 minutes.

6. Serve in a bowl, maybe with some fresh cilantro and a handful of pine nuts.

MACRONUTRIENTS PER SERVING: CALORIES: 421 FAT: 28 G CARBS: 7 G PROTEIN: 32 G

BRUSSELS SPROUTS
CHICKEN &
BACON SKILLET

Do you own a cast-iron skillet yet? This recipe is the perfect reason to invest in one. It creates a delicious, dare we say, addictive, crunch on anything you cook in it. The combination of cast-iron with these ingredients below is a match made especially for all you Cool Dudes.

INGREDIENTS

8 slices of bacon

1 pound (454 g) boneless & skinless chicken thighs

Sea salt, pepper & garlic powder

2 cups (200 g) brussels sprouts

4 tablespoons (60 ml) olive oil

½ cup (50 g) walnuts

WHAT TO DO

1. Cook bacon in a skillet until crispy and set aside, leaving the grease in the skillet.

2. Add chicken thighs to the skillet and season with an even layer of sea salt, pepper, and garlic powder. Flip after about 5 minutes.

3. While the chicken is cooking, chop Brussels sprouts and add them to the skillet with the chicken.

4. Everything is done when the chicken has browned and is firm to the touch (or when it reaches 165 F (74C) and the sprouts are soft.

5. Serve in a bowl with crumbled bacon, a drizzle of olive oil, and a small handful of chopped walnuts.

COOKING TIME:
20 MINS
SERVINGS:
4

MACRONUTRIENTS PER SERVING: CALORIES: 504   FAT: 38 G   CARBS: 7 G   PROTEIN: 37 G

CRAZY SALMON, VEGGIES, GUAC, AND SWEET POTATOES

This recipe did not make it into the book. We were just testing the color saturation and aspect ratio on the new camera. Yes, that's powdered sugar sprinkled on the sweet potatoes. Secret backstage reality TV style exposé in Brad's kitchen! Shhh, don't tell the keto police!

BUTTER
SALAD

Butter and pecans just go together; always have, always will. When combined with butter lettuce and salty chicken thighs, life really is a giant party.

INGREDIENTS

1 tablespoon (15 g) of ghee or butter (we really recommend butter since this is a "Butter Salad" but by all means, use ghee)

1 pound (454 g) boneless & skinless chicken thighs

Sea salt, pepper & garlic powder

8 cups (600 g) butter lettuce

⅓ cup (40 g) chopped pecans

WHAT TO DO

1. Melt ghee or butter in a skillet set to medium-high heat.

2. Add chicken thighs and cook, flipping after about 5 minutes.

3. The chicken is done when it has browned and is firm to the touch (or when it has reached 165F (74C).

4. Serve over a bed of butter lettuce and sprinkle with chopped pecans.

5. You can really make this amazing by melting a couple more tablespoons (30 g) of ghee or butter with some sea salt, pepper, and garlic powder and pouring it over your salad.

MACRONUTRIENTS PER SERVING: CALORIES: 286   FAT: 17 G   CARBS: 3 G   PROTEIN: 31 G

CHICKEN & VEGETABLE SOUP

Making soup is just about cooking layers of food with layers of seasonings. This chicken and vegetable soup uses zucchini instead of traditional carrot to keep the carb count low, and chicken thighs instead of breast to up that fat, man.

INGREDIENTS

1 tablespoon (15 g) ghee or butter

1 medium (160 g) onion

1 cup (225 g) celery

2 medium (400 g) zucchini

3 garlic cloves

1 pound (454 g) boneless & skinless chicken thighs

Sea salt & pepper

1 tablespoon (3 g) dried thyme

4 cups (1 liter) chicken bone broth or stock

WHAT TO DO

1. Add a tablespoon (15 g) of ghee or butter to a large pot set to medium heat.

2. Finely chop a peeled onion, celery, and the zucchini and add to the pot.

3. Add minced garlic and toss well with an even layer of sea salt and pepper.

4. Dice chicken and add to the pot, seasoning with some more sea salt and an even layer of dried thyme.

5. Add bone broth or stock and simmer on low heat, mostly covered, until the veggies are very soft and the chicken is cooked through, about 30 minutes.

COOKING TIME:
45 MINS
SERVINGS:
4

MACRONUTRIENTS PER SERVING: CALORIES: 312   FAT: 12 G   CARBS: 14 G   PROTEIN: 35 G

CREAMY CHICKEN & ZUCCHINI SALAD

When you don't have leftover chicken for this salad (go to detention), use canned; it's easy and gets the job done. Mince your scallion really well; it will mix with the simpler flavors from everything else nicely, adding a tasty punch for yo lunch. Sorry, not sorry about that.

INGREDIENTS

1 medium (220 g) zucchini

4 ounces (114 g) of leftover chicken or canned chicken packed in water

2 tablespoons (30 g) Primal Kitchen Avocado Oil Mayo

Sea salt, pepper & garlic powder

1 whole scallion, minced

½ medium (75 g) avocado

WHAT TO DO

1. Grate zucchini with a cheese grater, throwing away the top and end parts.

2. Chop up leftover chicken.

3. Mix mayo in a large bowl with a sprinkle of sea salt, pepper, and garlic powder.

4. Add the zucchini and chicken to the mayo and toss with minced scallion and diced avocado.

5. The zucchini will "sweat" excess water the more time it sits, so serve this immediately, maybe over a bed of your favorite lettuce.

MACRONUTRIENTS PER SERVING: CALORIES: 526 FAT: 40 G CARBS: 5 G PROTEIN: 34 G

DR. CATE'S SUPER
TESTOSTERONE BOOSTING STEW ⟶

While many foods have a scientifically validated testosterone boosting effect, Cool Dudes should never discount the importance of the psychological effects of food. In *Biology of Belief*, Dr. Bruce Lipton describes how your thoughts have a direct impact on your physiology. "Perception in your mind is reflected in the chemistry of your body; you can change the fate of your cells by altering your thoughts," Lipton explains. Positive thoughts cause mood-elevating hormones like serotonin and dopamine to flood the bloodstream, while negative thoughts spike stress hormones.

Dr. Cate reminds dudes that sexual arousal and ejaculations are parasympathetic functions. You need to be chill to perform. Feeling stressed, anxious, or insecure will mess up your mojo. This stew combines legit testosterone-boosting foods with an assortment of phallic foods to send good vibes your way during preparation and consumption.

INGREDIENTS

1 cucumber, wash thoroughly, peel, then massage the bare skin

2 carrots, wash, peel, then massage the bare skin

1 banana, peel slowly and carefully, one strand at a time.

1 pound (454 g) of stew meat, sliced in thick chunks

1 medium (160 g) onion

1 medium (123 g) tomato

1 6-ounce (150 g) can of tomato paste

2 cups (480 ml) of water

Sea salt

WHAT TO DO

1. Put the peeled cucumber and banana aside, since they would taste terrible in a stew.

2. Peel and chop the onion, carrots, and tomato and set aside.

3. In a skillet on medium heat, sear each side of the sliced meat for 1 minute, or until browned.

4. Add the chopped onion, chopped tomato, tomato paste, and water and reduce to a simmer until the meat is tender and the stew juices have thickened, about 15 minutes.

5. Season with sea salt to taste.

Dr. Cate's Super Testosterone Boosting Stew

Dr. Cate

MACRONUTRIENTS PER SERVING: CALORIES: 248 FAT: 12 G CARBS: 13 G PROTEIN: 22 G

KETO COOKING FOR COOL DUDES

Dude, if you keep these ingredients as staples in your kitchen, you'll win at life. Just sayin'.

FAST SALMON SALAD

INGREDIENTS

1 6-ounce (170 g) can of salmon (boneless and skinless or with bones and skin is fine)

2 tablespoons (30 g) mayonnaise

Sea salt & pepper

1 teaspoon (1 g) dried dill

1 teaspoon (2 g) dried curry powder

2 cups (150 g) mixed greens

WHAT TO DO

1. Toss mayo in a large bowl with all ingredients except mixed greens.

2. Arrange mixed greens on a plate and top with salmon mixture. Add some avocado for some extra fat.

COOKING TIME:
5 MINS

SERVING:
1

MACRONUTRIENTS PER SERVING: CALORIES: 522 FAT: 36 G CARBS: 8 G PROTEIN: 46 G

FRIED THIGHS WITH A BIG SIDE OF BROCCOLI

Chicken and broccoli dinners get a bad rap for being boring, so make this and prepare for it to blow your mind, because it's nothing short of decadent texture and flavor. Creamy and crispy, fatty and fresh. Follow our lead with some parsley and lemon zest as a garnish, and you'll be sending us thank-you letters…you're welcome in advance.

INGREDIENTS

1 pound (454 g) boneless and skinless chicken thighs

1 tablespoon (15 g) ghee or butter

Sea salt, pepper & garlic powder

1 teaspoon (1 g) dried dill

2 cups (140 g) broccoli

4 tablespoons (60 g) mayonnaise

Hot sauce

WHAT TO DO

1. Heat ghee or butter in a cast-iron skillet set to medium-high heat.

2. Add chicken thighs and sprinkle with sea salt, pepper, and garlic powder. Add dried dill and cook, covered with a piece of foil to keep from splattering.

3. While the chicken is cooking, steam broccoli florets.

4. Flip the chicken a few times with a metal spatula. It will begin to brown and its juices will thicken with the ghee and create brown bits in the pan. This is good! The chicken is done after about 12 minutes or when it has reached 165F (74C).

5. Serve on a plate (be sure to scrape up the bits in the pan) with a big side of broccoli and mayo with a splash of hot sauce mixed in. Make this more impressive with chopped fresh scallion or parsley as a garnish, or go all out and micro-grate some lemon zest over everything.

COOKING TIME: **20 MINS** SERVINGS: **4**

MACRONUTRIENTS PER SERVING: CALORIES: 334   FAT: 24 G   CARBS: 3 G   PROTEIN: 29 G

Turmeric has been used for quite some time as an anti-inflammatory spice. It's best absorbed by the body with some black pepper, so get in the habit of using these spices together. Add some good fat to this salad; we think avocado and green olives are nice ideas.

HOT CHOPPED SIRLOIN DINNER SALAD

INGREDIENTS

6 ounces (170 g) of sirloin

2 tablespoons (30 ml) olive oil

Sea salt, pepper & garlic powder

1 teaspoon (2 g) dried turmeric powder

1 tablespoon (15 ml) coconut aminos

2 cups (134 g) baby kale

COOKING TIME:
1-2 HOURS TO PREP, 10 MINUTES TO COOK
SERVINGS:
1

WHAT TO DO

1. Marinate sirloin in a shallow bowl with olive oil, sea salt, pepper, garlic powder, and dried turmeric for 1-2 hours before cooking. This will allow the sirloin to come to room temperature before cooking, which helps it cook evenly rather than searing fast on the outside and being raw and cold on the inside (unless you like that!).

2. When ready to cook, fire up your grill to high heat and cook for 3-4 minutes per side.

3. When done, transfer to a cutting board and dice in bite-sized pieces.

4. Layer over a bed of baby kale and dress with additional olive oil, sea salt, pepper, and a splash of coconut aminos.

MACRONUTRIENTS PER SERVING: CALORIES: 722   FAT: 52 G   CARBS: 13 G   PROTEIN: 50 G

KETO COOKING FOR COOL DUDES

KETO BREATH *SALAD*

If this doesn't get you blowing acetone, we don't know what will.

COOKING TIME:
15 MINS

SERVINGS:
1

INGREDIENTS

2 cups (200 g) of shredded cabbage

2 tablespoons (30 ml) of Pure C8 MCT Oil

1 tablespoon (15 g) of spicy brown mustard

1 large (100 g) Kiolbassa sausage

Seasonings/spices

Optional: chicharrones or crunchy cheese snack for crouton-like crunch

WHAT TO DO

1. On a grill, cook 1 large (100 g) Kiolbassa sausage. If you don't have a grill, cook in a stovetop cast-iron pan in a thin layer of water.

2. While the sausage is cooking, cut up roughly 2 cups (200 g) of cabbage thinly into shreds.

3. In a large mixing bowl, mix cabbage with 2 tablespoons (30 ml) of MCT oil, a large squirt of mustard, and a bit of spices and seasoning. Stir until cabbage starts to soften.

4. When the sausage is fully cooked, chop up and add to the mixing bowl with either chicharrones or crunchy cheese "croutons."

MACRONUTRIENTS PER SERVING: CALORIES: 429 FAT: 42 G CARBS: 8 G PROTEIN: 7 G

LIVER BURGER TRIANGLES

This unique offering was born from a failed attempt to make burger patties one day. The mixture was too squooshy, so the only choice was to spread it to cover the entire frying pan. Sure enough, the giant disk firmed up like a pancake, allowing for the cutting of pie-slice triangles!

INGREDIENTS

1.5 pounds (680 g) of ground buffalo, lamb, wagyu, or grass-fed beef

6 ounces (170 g) of chicken livers

Melted cheese (raw milk or other high-quality, aged cheese) to add onto the patties just before they're done

1 medium (150 g) avocado for topping the finished patties

WHAT TO DO

1. Melt a thin layer of butter on medium heat across a cast-iron or stainless steel skillet.

2. Puree the ground beef and the livers in Cuisinart or Ninja food processor. Spread the mixture across the entire pan, using a spatula to make it smooth and circular.

3. Cover the skillet and heat patiently on medium until the entire mixture starts to firm up.

4. Sprinkle with cheese near the end of the cooking time. Carve triangular slices with spatula edge and serve.

COOKING TIME:
25 MINS
SERVINGS:
6

MACRONUTRIENTS PER SERVING: CALORIES: 321 FAT: 16 G CARBS: 2 G PROTEIN: 28 G

MEDITERRANEAN SKILLET

If you don't already have a baking tray and some parchment paper, go out and buy them now and start making one-tray dinners tonight! Just layer everything on the tray, shake that salt and pepper over all your ingredients, bake, eat, and then crumple up the parchment and throw it away. Life is so easy, ain't it?

INGREDIENTS

1 pound (454 g) bone-in chicken thighs

1 tablespoon (15 g) ghee or butter

1 large (150 g) red bell pepper

Sea salt, pepper & garlic powder

1 tablespoon (2 g) dried Italian seasonings

10 (30 g) Kalamata olives

4 ounces (113 g) feta cheese

WHAT TO DO

1. Preheat your oven to 400F (204C).

2. Place chicken thighs on a baking tray lined with parchment paper.

3. Arrange sliced red bell peppers around the chicken.

4. Sprinkle with an even layer of sea salt, pepper, garlic powder, and Italian seasonings and bake until the chicken skin is browned or heated to 165F (74C) and the peppers have blistered, about 40 minutes.

5. Serve with Kalamata olives and feta cheese and liven it up with some fresh parsley and grated lemon zest.

COOKING TIME:
50 MINS
SERVINGS:
4

MACRONUTRIENTS PER SERVING: CALORIES: 394 FAT: 32 G CARBS: 4 G PROTEIN: 21 G

PRESTO PESTO
SCALLOPS

This seems like a gourmet meal, but the whole thing can be made in 10 minutes or so. This can also be used as an appetizer for when you are invited to a party and asked to bring appetizers. Just get some toothpicks and everyone can have a scallop.

INGREDIENTS

1 pound (454 g) of scallops. Find frozen at Trader Joe's or big box store, or fresh at a fish market or quality grocer. You can use large or baby scallops—large recommended

1 bunch or small plastic container (.66 ounce/18 g) of fresh basil

½ cup (70 g) of pine nuts

⅓ cup (80 ml) of extra-virgin domestic olive oil

1 tablespoon (15 ml) of lemon juice

1 tablespoon (15 g) of butter

Assorted spices

Optional: sun-dried tomatoes, ½ medium (80 g) onion, pureed

WHAT TO DO

1. Puree the basil and pine nuts.

2. Add olive oil, gradually, as you puree to achieve the desired consistency of store-bought pestos made with disgusting canola oil. Shame on the otherwise super cool Costco Kirkland brand!

3. Add lemon juice, desired spices, and any optional ingredients. Right now, the clock is at probably two minutes.

4. Rinse the scallops in warm water and make sure there is no residual ice.

5. Heat the butter in a cast-iron skillet on medium-high. When the butter is melted, carefully place the scallops into the skillet so each has a clean application of one side to the bottom of the skillet.

6. After around 90 seconds, flip each scallop individually to cook the other side. The end goal is to have a nice browning of the sides and a soft middle. Since you eat scallops raw at the sushi bar, please err on the undercooked side rather than turning your expensive scallops into rubber canine chew toys.

7. After cooking the second side, throw the scallops into the pesto mixture and stir well. This is best served immediately while the scallops are warm.

Note: If you are using baby scallops, continually churn the scallops instead of following the big scallop directions.

MACRONUTRIENTS PER SERVING: CALORIES: 419   FAT: 33 G   CARBS: 12 G   PROTEIN: 25 G

KETO COOKING FOR COOL DUDES

Radicchio
ROAST BEEF CUPS

Ok, full disclosure. Make these as lettuce cups only if you really like to have your meal served in lettuce cups or if you're serving them to people who do. If not, just chop everything up together and pat yourself on the back. Good job, lunch is served!

INGREDIENTS

8 radicchio leaves

4 ounces (113 g) deli roast beef slices

2 pickles

1 tablespoon (15 g) yellow mustard

1 medium (150 g) avocado or 2 tablespoons (30 g) Primal Kitchen Avocado Oil Mayo

WHAT TO DO

1. Separate radicchio leaves (the leaves will separate easier if you slice off the tough bottom end of the radicchio first).

2. Place a couple of slices of roast beef in each leaf and garnish with some minced pickle, mustard, and either avocado or mayonnaise (or a bit of both!).

MACRONUTRIENTS PER SERVING: CALORIES: 54   FAT: 4 G   CARBS: 1 G   PROTEIN: 4 G

KETO COOKING FOR COOL DUDES

RICE & SAUSAGE BOWL

We're thanking our lucky stars that it's getting easier and easier to find foods like cauliflower rice at grocery stores. Sure, you can make it yourself, and please do, if you need "ricing cauliflower" on your resume, but in a pinch, the bagged is nice.

INGREDIENTS

1 16-ounce (454 g) bag of cauliflower rice

2 tablespoons (30 g) ghee or butter

Sea salt, pepper & garlic powder

2 fully cooked chicken sausage links

2 cups (60 g) spinach

2 tablespoons (10 g) Parmesan cheese

WHAT TO DO

1. Heat a tablespoon (15 g) of butter or ghee in a skillet on medium heat.

2. Add cauliflower rice, seasoning with an even layer of sea salt, pepper, and garlic powder and stirring often until the cauliflower is soft, about 3 minutes.

3. Transfer the cauliflower rice to another dish, and in the same skillet with another tablespoon (15 g) of ghee or butter, cook chicken sausage until the skin is seared and heated through.

4. Add a big handful of spinach to the skillet, turn off the heat, and let it wilt.

5. Serve sausage and spinach over cauliflower rice with Parmesan.

MACRONUTRIENTS PER SERVING: CALORIES: 325 FAT: 24 G CARBS: 14 G PROTEIN: 19 G

ROAST BEEF & AVOCADO BOWL

Lunch can be as easy as chopping up this roast beef and avocado bowl, or even easier if you disregard the directions and just add the ingredients to a bowl and use your kitchen scissors to slice and dice your way to a satisfying no-cook meal break.

INGREDIENTS

4 ounces (114 g) deli roast beef

1 medium (150 g) avocado

2 tablespoons (14 g) sun-dried tomatoes

Sea salt & pepper

1 tablespoon (15 g) of Primal Kitchen Avocado Oil Mayo

WHAT TO DO

1. Chop roast beef, avocado, and sun-dried tomatoes on a cutting board.

2. Add to a bowl and toss with sea salt and pepper.

3. Consume right from the bowl with mayo.

4. Make this bowl a little more impressive with some minced radish and fresh parsley.

COOKING TIME:
5 MINS
SERVINGS:
1

MACRONUTRIENTS PER SERVING: CALORIES: 517 FAT: 40 G CARBS: 6 G PROTEIN: 30 G

KETO COOKING FOR COOL DUDES

It's recipes like this that make life worth living and this book worth writing. If you've been working hard all morning and ready for a short break, or you're home late and not into preparing a gourmet dinner, this colorful and creative meal can be made in a few minutes.

SARDINES 'N
SUN-DRIED

INGREDIENTS

2 4.4 ounce-tins (125 g) of sardines packed in olive oil

3 tablespoons (21 g) of sun-dried tomatoes (make sure your brand isn't swimming in bad oils)

1 ounce (28 g) of walnuts

WHAT TO DO

1. Heat a skillet with a little butter and add the sardines and sun-dried tomatoes. Stir fry.

2. Once cooked, crush the walnuts in your hand and sprinkle on top. A tablespoon (15 g) of Primal Kitchen Chipotle Lime Mayo or Green Goddess Dressing works well here, too.

COOKING TIME:
5 MINS
SERVINGS:
1

MACRONUTRIENTS PER SERVING: CALORIES: 430 FAT: 26 G CARBS: 14 G PROTEIN: 35 G

SARDINE SALAD

Sardines are packed with calcium, iron, potassium, omega-3's, and even Vitamin D, which is rarer to find in food. Keep a bunch of sardine cans in your pantry and you'll always be ready to prep a nutritious meal.

INGREDIENTS

1 4.4-ounce (125 g) of sardines packed in olive oil

Sea salt, pepper & garlic powder

2 cups (60 g) spinach

5 cherry tomatoes

1 ounce (28 g) of walnuts

WHAT TO DO

1. Add sardines and the olive oil they are packed in into a bowl and toss with sea salt (leave out if the sardines are salty enough for you), pepper, and a sprinkle of garlic powder.

2. Chop spinach, halve cherry tomatoes, and toss together with the sardines with a small handful of walnuts.

3. Serve in a bowl.

COOKING TIME:
10 MINS
SERVINGS:
1

MACRONUTRIENTS PER SERVING: CALORIES: 397   FAT: 24 G   CARBS: 9 G   PROTEIN: 39 G

SEARED STRIP STEAKS WITH BACON & MUSHROOMS

Steak, bacon, and mushrooms—you'll win every time if you keep this trio in your fridge and ready to cook up when you want another visit to flavor town. Use this as a base recipe and add other herbs and spices such as rosemary or smoked paprika if you like.

INGREDIENTS

1 6-ounce (170 g) strip steak

1 tablespoon (15 ml) olive or avocado oil

Sea salt, pepper & garlic powder

½ teaspoon (2 g) dried red pepper flakes

2 slices bacon

1 cup (75 g) cremini mushrooms

WHAT TO DO

1. Marinate strip steak in olive or avocado oil, sea salt, pepper. garlic powder, and dried red pepper flakes for about an hour before cooking.

2. Cook bacon in a skillet set to medium heat until crispy and set aside.

3. In the same skillet, add the mushrooms (slice if you want or keep them whole) and cook in the bacon grease until they begin to soften, about 3–5 minutes.

4. Scrape the mushrooms to the side of the skillet and place the strip steak directly in the skillet, allowing it to sear by not moving it as it cooks, about 2 minutes per side.

5. Serve steak, mushrooms, and bacon on a big plate. Add some avocado and fresh herbs for some extra fat and flavor.

COOKING TIME:
1 HOUR TO PREP, 20 MINUTES
SERVINGS:
1

MACRONUTRIENTS PER SERVING: CALORIES: 414   FAT: 25 G   CARBS: 2 G   PROTEIN: 46 G

A Bigass midday salad has been the centerpiece of the primal/paleo movement since Mark Sisson first showed YouTube visitors how to make a colorful, nutrient-dense salad in two minutes in 2008. With morning fasting such a popular strategy for fat reduction and cellular repair, a midday salad is an ideal way to break the fast and ensure you meet your varied nutritional needs, especially your daily dose of vegetables. While a salad is generally comprised of a bunch of vegetable carbohydrates and a protein source like steak, chicken, or fish, dousing it with tons of healthy dressing—made with extra-virgin olive oil or avocado oil like Primal Kitchen products—makes it a high-fat, keto-aligned meal.

INGREDIENTS

3 cups (225 g) of lettuce or mixed greens as a base

4 ounces (113 g) chopped meat: steak, chicken, turkey, salmon, smoked salmon, sardines, or pass if you are vegan (there's enough other cool stuff in here)

1 hard-boiled egg (chopped up to sprinkle on top, helps for Instagram photo shoots)

12 cherry tomatoes

1 medium (50 g) diced celery stalk

½ cup (50 g) cucumber

1 tablespoon (6 g) minced onion

1 medium (60 g) diced carrot

Suggested: ½ cup (113 g) Trader Joe's Mango Jicama Slaw

1 ounce (28 g) nuts: walnuts, pecans, cashews, pine nuts, either whole or ground up in your Ninja

½ medium (75 g) sliced avocado: monounsaturated fat powerhouse takes any salad from good to awesome

½ cup (25 g) blueberries or pomegranate seeds when they are in season; sprinkle a few on there. A pinch of dried goji berries is cool, too

2 tablespoons (30 ml) Primal Kitchen avocado oil-based salad dressing or homemade extra-virgin olive oil and lemon preparation

SISSON BIG ASS SALAD

WHAT TO DO

1. In a large bowl, toss all ingredients, saving the hard-boiled egg for last to sprinkle on top as a better idea than stale croutons.

2. Use this recipe as a suggestion and get creative adding different greens, proteins and lower-carb fruits to your salad. The sky is the limit!

COOKING TIME:
10 MINS
SERVINGS:
1

(1 serving = 4 ounces of steak, ½ cup of a Trader Joe's Mango Jicama Slaw, 12 cherry tomatoes, 1 carrot, 1 celery stalk, 1 ounce of walnuts, ½ avocado, ¼ cup blueberries, 2 Tbs. Primal Kitchen Greek Vinaigrette)

MACRONUTRIENTS PER SERVING: CALORIES: 863   FAT: 58 G   CARBS: 52 G   PROTEIN: 42 G

SKILLET
CABBAGE & BEEF

Oh, all the things you can cook up with a pound of ground beef! Keep blocks of it in your freezer and don't forget to defrost it when you plan to cook it; otherwise, all you can boast of is how much ground beef is in your freezer, which isn't that cool.

INGREDIENTS

1 pound (454 g) of ground beef

4 cups (400 g) of shredded cabbage

Sea salt, pepper & garlic powder

2 tablespoons (30 ml) coconut aminos

WHAT TO DO

1. Add ground beef to a skillet set to medium heat, breaking up with a wooden spoon.

2. When the beef is just about cooked through, add the shredded cabbage and cook until soft, about 5 minutes.

3. Season with sea salt, pepper, and garlic powder.

4. Drain excess grease and water from the skillet and add a splash of coconut aminos to the skillet before serving.

COOKING TIME:
15 MINS
SERVINGS:
4

MACRONUTRIENTS PER SERVING: CALORIES: 225   FAT: 14 G   CARBS: 6 G   PROTEIN: 23 G

KETO COOKING FOR COOL DUDES

This salad has endless possibilities, use it as a base recipe and fancy it up with your favorite fixings. We like this with extra-sharp cheddar because it's so good. But hey, what do we know about what cheese you think is good? You've trusted us thus far, we trust you, too!

SMOKED TURKEY
& CHEESE BOWL

INGREDIENTS

4 ounces (113 g) smoked deli turkey breast

1 ounce (28 g) extra-sharp cheddar cheese

2 tablespoons (30 ml) olive oil

Sea salt & pepper

½ teaspoon (2 g) dried red pepper flakes

2 cups (150 g) arugula

WHAT TO DO

1. Chop smoked deli turkey and cheese on a cutting board and layer it over a bed of arugula.

2. Drizzle with olive oil and sprinkle with sea salt, pepper, and dried red pepper flakes.

3. Feel free to add other tasty toppings such as sun-dried tomatoes, olives, or avocado.

COOKING TIME:
5 MINS
SERVINGS:
1

MACRONUTRIENTS PER SERVING: CALORIES: 459   FAT: 36 G   CARBS: 1 G   PROTEIN: 32 G

CARNIVORE ENTRÉES

The following section proves that carnivore is more than a "hamburger and steak every day, every meal" craze that some naysayers characterize it as with a dismissive scoff. These recipes were contributed by young carnivore advocate **William Shewfelt**, who joins Brad and Brian as a co-author on *Carnivore Cooking for Cool Dudes*. Will specializes in coaching people to drop excess body fat by following a carnivore eating pattern and a sensible blend of comfortable cardio and high-intensity weight training at PrimalBody.co.

WILL
...you be able

...to look like Will if you eat these recipes? *Absolutely!*

BACON-WRAPPED MEATBALLS

This recipe includes pork and some non-carnivore seasonings, so if you don't tolerate seasonings well, best to stick to pink salt.

INGREDIENTS

1 pound (454 g) of ground pork

1 pound (454 g) of ground beef

1 egg, beaten

¼ cup (25 g) of grated Parmesan

Italian seasonings

Garlic powder

Himalayan pink salt

Black pepper

Primal Kitchen Classic BBQ Sauce

16-18 bacon slices, cut in half

WHAT TO DO

1. Preheat the oven to 350F (175C).

2. Put ground pork and ground beef in bowl. Add beaten egg. Then add Parmesan, Italian seasonings, garlic, pink salt, and black pepper in bowl. Mix ingredients together well.

3. Line a baking sheet with foil and place a non-stick baking rack on top of it.

4. Form the meat into meatballs. Wrap the meat in bacon strips and place the bacon-wrapped meatballs on the rack.

5. Bake for 15 minutes.

6. Apply the Primal Kitchen barbecue sauce.

7. Bake for another 15 minutes.

8. Serve immediately.

COOKING TIME:
40 MINS
SERVINGS:
8

(8 SERVINGS, 32 MEATBALLS, 16 SLICES OF BACON)
MACRONUTRIENTS PER SERVING: CALORIES: 345   FAT: 26 G   CARBS: 1 G   PROTEIN: 27 G

CARNIVORE MUSCLE BOWL

The Muscle Bowl is Shewfelt's personal favorite simple and delicious carnivore meal. "It ain't pretty...but it's damn good. It's quick, simple, and will keep you lean...all while being absolutely delicious. Eat up! No anti-nutrients here," he explains.

INGREDIENTS

Himalayan pink salt

1 pound (454 g) of ground beef

4 eggs

1 cup (55 g) of canned salmon or 1 4.4 ounce-tin (125 g) of sardines

Shredded cheese

COOKING TIME:
20 MINS
SERVINGS:
4

WHAT TO DO

1. Heat a medium-sized pan to medium heat. Add 1 pound (454 g) of ground beef and use a spatula to separate it and spread it out evenly across the pan. Add salmon or sardines.

2. Generously add Himalayan pink salt. Put a lid on the pan and turn to medium-low for 5-7 minutes, occasionally using spatula to move the ground beef around and cook evenly.

3. Add 4 whole eggs. Add more pink salt. Stir the eggs into the beef. As the egg begins to set on the bottom, use the spatula to flip it in the pan and swirl the liquid egg portions around to evenly cook.

4. When the beef and egg mixture is set, slide the entire mixture into a straining bowl over the sink. Allow the excess fat and liquid to drain into the sink. Then put the beef-egg-fish mixture back into the pan.

5. Slide the food onto a plate using a spatula and add shredded cheese on top. Serve immediately.

MACRONUTRIENTS PER SERVING: CALORIES: 372 FAT: 24 G CARBS: 1 G PROTEIN: 39 G

KETO COOKING FOR COOL DUDES

GRILLED *SHRIMP*

This recipe for grilled shrimp takes just minutes to prepare and captures the flavors of summer no matter when you make them. Aim to find high-quality shrimp whenever you can, fresh if you can, but frozen is great.

INGREDIENTS

1 pound (454 g) tail-on, wild-caught shrimp

Sea salt & pepper

1 teaspoon (2 g) smoked paprika

1 tablespoon (15 g) ghee or butter

WHAT TO DO

1. Toss shrimp in a bowl with sea salt, pepper, and an even layer of smoked paprika.

2. Fire up your grill (or cast-iron skillet) to high heat and place shrimp on the hot grill, being careful not to move the shrimp once they're on.

3. Cook for 1 minute per side. The shrimp will brighten and deepen in color once done.

4. Serve immediately, maybe with a side of Creamy Cauliflower Grits (page 151) and a sprinkle of dried red pepper flakes.

MACRONUTRIENTS PER SERVING: CALORIES: 115   FAT: 5 G   CARBS: 3 G   PROTEIN: 19 G

Another creative carnivore category recipe that will get you carnivore shredded. Shewfelt explains to dudes, "Steaks can drive your grocery bill up, and plain burgers can get old real fast—so try this to spice up an old classic."

MUSTARD BACON BURGERS

INGREDIENTS

1 pound (454 g) of ground beef

4 ounces (113 g) of bacon, diced

Himalayan pink salt

Black pepper

4 teaspoons (20 g) of yellow mustard

COOKING TIME:
20 MINS
SERVINGS:
2

WHAT TO DO

1. Heat a pan to medium-high and cook bacon in the pan until crispy. Leave the bacon grease in the pan and put the bacon bits into a bowl with the ground beef. Season with pink salt and black pepper and mix together.

2. Form the ground beef into 4 burger patties.

3. Sear the burgers in the pan on high heat. Cook for 2 minutes, then flip the patties and cook for 2 more minutes.

4. Once cooked, apply 1 teaspoon (5 g) of mustard to each of the burger patties—flip the patties and let them sear in the mustard for 30 seconds. Serve immediately.

MACRONUTRIENTS PER SERVING: CALORIES: 502 FAT: 34 G CARBS: 1 G PROTEIN: 48 G

SEARED
SIMPLE LAMB CHOPS

These lamb chops are perfect to dip in **Eggplant Tahini Dip (page 182)** or to debone and serve on a salad with **Basil Curry Vinaigrette (page 169)**. Lamb is fed with grass, so you'll be getting some good omega-3's every time you whip these babies up.

INGREDIENTS

8 lamb chops

2 tablespoons (30 g) ghee or butter

Sea salt, pepper & garlic powder

WHAT TO DO

1. Set lamb chops in a shallow dish and rub them with ghee or butter, sea salt, pepper, and garlic powder for about an hour before you plan to cook them.

2. Fire up your grill or heat a cast-iron skillet to high heat.

3. Place chops on the hot grill or skillet and sear for about 1 minute per side if the chops are thin, 2 if they are thicker.

COOKING TIME:
1 HOUR TO PREP, 10 MINS
SERVINGS:
4

MACRONUTRIENTS PER SERVING: CALORIES: 368 FAT: 28 G CARBS: 0 G PROTEIN: 30 G

STEAK AND OYSTERS

Shewfelt's steak and oysters pack a major nutritional punch and they taste amazing. They may even confer some extracurricular benefits (aphrodisiac anyone?) but enough about that...let's get cooking.

INGREDIENTS

1 New York strip steak

1 3-ounce tin (85 g) of oysters

Himalayan pink salt

Black pepper

Primal Kitchen Steak Sauce

WHAT TO DO

1. Heat the grill to high. Liberally salt the steak with Himalayan pink salt and black pepper.

2. Place the steak on the grill for 4 to 5 minutes or until it starts to brown and is slightly charred.

3. Open the tin of oysters and carefully place them on the grill near the steak.

4. Flip the steak and continue to grill for 3–5 minutes.

5. Flip the oysters after 1 minute and grill for 1 more minute.

6. Serve immediately with Primal Kitchen Steak Sauce.

COOKING TIME:
10 MINS
SERVINGS:
2

(2 SERVINGS WITH 1 8-OUNCE STEAK AND 1 60-GRAM TIN OF OYSTERS)
MACRONUTRIENTS PER SERVING: CALORIES: 379 FAT: 26 G CARBS: 6 G PROTEIN: 28 G

BLISTERED
CHERRY
TOMATOES

When you find a recipe easier than this (fasting doesn't count!), will you let us know? If you want to make this more complicated to up your cool factor, find a faraway farm, pick your own cherry tomatoes, and roast them over an open fire (mmm!) and invite us over to share, please?

INGREDIENTS

1 pound (454 g) cherry tomatoes

WHAT TO DO

1. Preheat oven to 400F (204C).

2. Place cherry tomatoes on a baking tray lined with parchment paper and roast in the oven until they are blistered, about 25 minutes.

3. Use to garnish everything! Scrambles, salads, and dinner plates.

COOKING
TIME:
30 MINS
SERVINGS:
4

MACRONUTRIENTS PER SERVING: CALORIES: 20   FAT: 0 G   CARBS: 4 G   PROTEIN: 1 G

BROCCOLI BACON
AVOCADO MASH

When you're craving something creamy and fatty and don't care about anything else, you'll know you have gone keto. This recipe is delicious just on its own and is also wonderful topped on a salad or with some grilled meats. Add some dried red pepper flakes if you prefer a bit of heat.

INGREDIENTS

4 slices of bacon

1 medium (160 g) onion

Sea salt, pepper & garlic powder

1 16-ounce bag (454 g) of broccoli

2 medium (300 g) avocado

WHAT TO DO

1. Cook bacon in a skillet until crispy and set aside, leaving the grease in the pan.

2. Peel and chop an onion and add it to the skillet with an even layer of sea salt, pepper, and garlic powder.

3. Add chopped broccoli and toss everything together with a metal spatula until it has all softened and begins to caramelize.

4. Transfer to a food processor and pulse with avocados until everything is creamy.

5. Serve with crumbled bacon.

COOKING TIME: **15 MINS**
SERVINGS: **4**

MACRONUTRIENTS PER SERVING: CALORIES: 208   FAT: 16 G   CARBS: 9 G   PROTEIN: 8 G

Cheesy BROCCOLI RICE

Cheese and broccoli are as old as time and never old at the same time....that makes sense, right? We're partial to extra-sharp cheddar cheese, but mix it up and go wild with whatever cheese fits your fancy.

INGREDIENTS

1 tablespoon (15 g) ghee or butter

1 16-ounce (454 g) bag of broccoli rice

Sea salt, pepper & garlic powder

1 cup (125 g) grated raw or extra sharp cheddar cheese

Fresh scallion or parsley

WHAT TO DO

1. Add ghee or butter to a skillet set to medium-high heat.

2. Add broccoli rice, sea salt, pepper, and an even layer of garlic powder.

3. Stir often, uncovered, until broccoli is soft, about 3 minutes.

4. Stir in grated cheese and serve with minced scallion or parsley (or both!).

MACRONUTRIENTS PER SERVING: CALORIES: 149 FAT: 5 G CARBS: 6 G PROTEIN: 6 G

BACON 'N BRUSSELS

You can probably copy this recipe by sight, like Mozart on the piano. Cook the bacon first! Watch the Brussels carefully so they are cooked just right with a little crunch. No Cool Dude wants to eat, touch, or look at softie Brussels sprouts (see Dr. Cate's comments on page 94).

CREAMY ALMOND BUTTER
& SAGE GREEN BEANS

You often see almond butter paired with high-fructose fruits, but try it in a savory veggie dish with sage and coconut aminos and you'll be, like, bye–bye, sugary snackies!

INGREDIENTS

½ cup (75 g) French green beans

2 tablespoons (30 g) almond butter

Sea salt, pepper & garlic powder

1 teaspoon (1 g) dried sage

1 tablespoon (15 ml) coconut aminos

WHAT TO DO

1. Steam green beans until tender, about 5-7 minutes.

2. While green beans are steaming, add a big scoop of almond butter (creamy or crunchy), sea salt, pepper, garlic powder, dried sage, and coconut aminos to a bowl and stir well.

3. Add steamed green beans to the bowl and toss until the almond butter coats all of the green beans.

MACRONUTRIENTS PER SERVING: CALORIES: 243   FAT: 18 G   CARBS: 14 G   PROTEIN: 7 G

CREAMY CAULIFLOWER GRITS

We think this recipe is more involved because you need a blender to make it, but we also think this recipe for creamy cauliflower grits will knock your socks off and make you kiss your blender thank you. A pinch of nutmeg really brings this dish together; you can find it in the spice aisle at your grocery market.

INGREDIENTS

8 slices of bacon

1 16-ounce (454 g) bag of cauliflower rice

2 tablespoons (30 g) ghee or butter

Sea salt & pepper

2 garlic cloves

½ cup (120 ml) unsweetened almond milk

Pinch of dried ground nutmeg

WHAT TO DO

1. Cook bacon in a skillet set to medium heat until crispy and set aside, leaving the grease in the pan.

2. Add cauliflower rice, ghee or butter, sea salt, pepper, and peeled and minced garlic cloves.

3. Stir often until soft, about 3 minutes.

4. Remove from the skillet and add to a blender with almond milk and a pinch of ground nutmeg.

5. Blend until creamy and serve in a shallow bowl with bits of crumbled bacon. Kick this up a notch with some fresh parsley, and make it a more complete meal with some Grilled Shrimp (page 135).

COOKING TIME:
20 MINS
SERVINGS:
4

MACRONUTRIENTS PER SERVING: CALORIES: 171   FAT: 15 G   CARBS: 4 G   PROTEIN: 7 G

GRILLED ZUCCHINI

There are some things in life that everyone needs to learn, such as saying "please" and "thank you" and grilling up a bunch of fresh zucchini. Get real fancy with this and garnish it with fresh basil and feta cheese or some toasted pistachios and sliced almonds.

INGREDIENTS

4 medium (800 g) zucchini

2 tablespoons (30 ml) olive oil

Sea salt, pepper & garlic powder

1 tablespoon (2 g) dried basil

Lemon

WHAT TO DO

1. Fire up your grill or a grill pan set to high heat.

2. Cut zucchini in long pieces by slicing in half, lengthwise, then cut the halves in 4 long slices. One zucchini will yield 8 slices.

3. Brush with olive oil and sprinkle with sea salt, pepper, garlic powder, and dried basil.

4. Grill, only flipping it as needed, until it is soft, and has dark grill lines on each piece.

5. Serve with fresh lemon zest. (A micro plane zester is easiest for this; you could also peel a piece of the lemon skin and mince it, but that is more work.)

COOKING TIME:
15 MINS
SERVINGS:
4

MACRONUTRIENTS PER SERVING: CALORIES: 96   FAT: 7 G   CARBS: 7 G   PROTEIN: 3 G

Why is Moroccan food so good; and if you haven't tried it, why not? Maybe it's because Moroccan recipes do a fantastic job at combining flavors, such as savory from garlic and turmeric and sweet from cinnamon. Practice being cool by experimenting with spices. This recipe is a good place to begin.

COOKING TIME:
15 MINS
SERVINGS:
4

MOROCCAN
CAULI RICE

INGREDIENTS

1 16-ounce (454 g) bag of cauliflower rice

1 medium (160 g) onion

1 tablespoon (15 g) ghee or butter

Sea salt, pepper & garlic powder

1 tablespoon (7 g) dried turmeric powder

1 teaspoon (2 g) ground cinnamon

WHAT TO DO

1. Heat a tablespoon (15 g) of butter or ghee in a skillet set to medium heat.

2. Add a peeled and chopped onion (white or yellow works well) and cook, stirring often, until the onion is soft, about 5 minutes.

3. Add cauliflower rice, seasoning with an even layer of sea salt, pepper, and garlic powder and stirring often until the cauliflower is soft, about 3 minutes.

4. Season with turmeric powder and cinnamon.

5. Make this fancy by garnishing with fresh parsley and sliced almonds.

MACRONUTRIENTS PER SERVING: CALORIES: 73 FAT: 4 G CARBS: 7 G PROTEIN: 3 G

ROASTED CAULIFLOWER STEAKS

We're not going to try and convince you that cauliflower is steak, despite us calling this recipe so, but we will try to convince you to cook your cauliflower with as much passion as this recipe calls for. But since we're on the topic of steak, it would go perfectly with this dish. Just sayin'.

INGREDIENTS

1 large (840 g) head of cauliflower

2 tablespoons (30 g) ghee or butter

Sea salt, pepper & garlic powder

1 tablespoon (7 g) dried smoked paprika

2 tablespoons (30 g) tahini

WHAT TO DO

1. Preheat oven to 400F (204C).

2. Slice cauliflower as if you're cutting thick slices of bread (don't get lost in the fantasy) and arrange on a baking tray lined with parchment paper.

3. Rub with ghee or butter and season with sea salt, pepper, and an even layer of garlic powder and smoked paprika.

4. Roast in the oven until soft and caramelized, about 20-25 minutes.

5. Serve with a drizzle of tahini, and to make it look more impressive, add some grated lemon zest and fresh parsley.

COOKING TIME:
30 MINS
SERVINGS:
4

MACRONUTRIENTS PER SERVING: CALORIES: 153   FAT: 12 G   CARBS: 9 G   PROTEIN: 4 G

Fennel is a delicious vegetable that a lot of people haven't tried, so break the mold and get this on your menu, stat! Fennel aids in digestion and boosts immunity. If you like eating fennel, you'll probably like drinking it as a tea, which you can find in the tea section at most health food markets.

ROASTED FENNEL

INGREDIENTS

3 (270 g) fennel bulbs

2 tablespoons (30 g) ghee or butter

Sea salt, pepper & garlic powder

1 tablespoon (15ml) balsamic vinegar

Parsley

WHAT TO DO

1. Preheat oven to 400F (204C).

2. Chop fennel bulbs and arrange on a baking tray lined with parchment paper.

3. Place several bits of ghee or butter on fennel and sprinkle with sea salt, pepper, and an even layer of garlic powder.

4. Roast in oven for about 5 minutes and then toss to distribute the ghee or butter.

5. Add balsamic vinegar, toss once more, then finish baking for 20–25 minutes, or until fennel is soft and caramelized.

6. Serve with minced parsley.

COOKING TIME:
30 MINS
SERVINGS:
4

MACRONUTRIENTS PER SERVING: CALORIES: 96 FAT: 8 G CARBS: 6 G PROTEIN: 1 G

SIMPLEST LOW-CARB FRIED RICE

We kept this recipe for low-carb fried rice simple, because we don't need things to be too fancy to be really tasty. But if you're the fancy type, add in some freshly grated ginger, a little shredded carrot, and toasted dried coconut.

INGREDIENTS

1 16-ounce (454 g) bag of cauliflower rice

1 tablespoon (15 ml) toasted sesame oil

Sea salt, pepper & garlic powder

4 cups (400 g) shredded cabbage

1 egg

Scallion

2 tablespoons (30 ml) coconut aminos

WHAT TO DO

1. Heat a tablespoon (15 ml) of sesame oil in a skillet set to medium heat.

2. Add cauliflower rice, seasoning with an even layer of sea salt, pepper, and garlic powder and stirring often until the cauliflower is soft, about 3 minutes.

3. Add shredded cabbage to the skillet and toss.

4. Crack an egg onto the cauliflower and cabbage mix and break up by scrambling everything together.

5. Stir in a minced scallion and a splash of coconut aminos and enjoy.

COOKING TIME:
15 MINS
SERVINGS:
4

MACRONUTRIENTS PER SERVING: CALORIES: 76   FAT: 5 G   CARBS: 10 G   PROTEIN: 4 G

SNACKS
&TREATS

Almond butter is amazing on chicken. The end. Really, the next time you need a little something to tide you over, give this combo a try. It's sweet, salty, and creamy and really hits the spot.

ALMOND BUTTER
CHICKEN

INGREDIENTS

1 6-ounce package (170 g) of deli chicken slices

2 tablespoons (30 g) almond butter

Sea salt & pepper

½ cup (50 g) blueberries

WHAT TO DO

1. Mix almond butter in a bowl with a sprinkle of sea salt and pepper.

2. Fold in blueberries.

3. Place chicken slices (you could use turkey, too) on a cutting board and place a small spoonful of the almond butter and blueberry mix onto each meat center.

4. Flatten a little and roll up.

COOKING TIME:
10 MINS
SERVINGS:
2

MACRONUTRIENTS PER SERVING: CALORIES: 201   FAT: 11 G   CARBS: 9 G   PROTEIN: 20 G

This snack is like eating a little piece of summer vacation set sail on the Italian seas. So if that sounds like a good time, make these up as soon as possible. If you really don't care about the whole boat thing, just chop everything up on a big cutting board and serve as a salad. Equally good.

ANTIPASTI SNACK BOATS

INGREDIENTS

2 (170 g) heads of endive

10 (30 g) Kalamata olives

2 tablespoons (14 g) sun-dried tomatoes

¼ cup (5 g) fresh basil

1 large (150 g) yellow or red bell pepper

WHAT TO DO

1. Separate endive leaves and set aside.

2. Mince olives, sun-dried tomatoes, basil, and bell pepper all together on a cutting board.

3. Fill leaves and arrange on a serving platter for your next party, garnishing with some fresh parsley if you really want to look cool.

COOKING TIME:
10 MINS
SERVINGS:
4

MACRONUTRIENTS PER SERVING: CALORIES: 56 FAT: 3 G CARBS: 7 G PROTEIN: 2 G

BASIL CURRY VINAIGRETTE

COOKING TIME:
5 MINS
SERVINGS:
8

This vinaigrette is so good, don't limit serving it with only salads. Use it as a dip for veggies or a marinade for meats. Cilantro tastes nice if you don't have basil. Or go crazy and use a bit of both!

INGREDIENTS

1 cup (240 ml) olive oil

Sea salt & pepper

2 garlic cloves

1 cup (20 g) fresh basil

4 tablespoons (60 ml) lemon juice or apple cider vinegar

1 tablespoon (7 g) dried curry powder

WHAT TO DO

1. Add olive oil, salt, pepper, garlic cloves, basil leaves, lemon juice or apple cider vinegar, and curry powder to a high-speed blender.

2. Blend until creamy, adding olive oil as needed. If it's not blending easily or it looks too thin, add some olive oil.

3. Serve over salads or use as a marinade for meats.

4. Store in the fridge for up to a week.

MACRONUTRIENTS PER SERVING: CALORIES: 245   FAT: 27 G   CARBS: 1 G   PROTEIN: 0 G

BRAD'S
DELICIOUS
WHITE BALLS

COOKING TIME:
10 MINS TO PREP & 30-60 MINS TO CHILL
SERVINGS:
12

A unique and satisfying snack on the go or dessert option for top athletes winning major titles. And you. Depending on your level of appreciation for coconut, feel free to back off a bit on the three coconut ingredients and add more nut butter to the mixing bowl. When you've mixed the ingredients and are forming the balls, don't be discouraged if they seem crumbly. And yes, your hands will get greasy.

If the mixture is too liquidy to even form a ball, add a bit more mixed nuts and/or almond/coconut flour until you can form a proper ball. Don't worry, they will firm up nicely after a brief stint in the fridge and then stabilize when stored at room temp. You don't need much sweetener if you add nut butters. Just mix the ingredients until you get desired pasty consistency in the bowl, then form the balls. Brad is so comfortable manipulating his balls that he doesn't even measure out stuff anymore.

INGREDIENTS

1 cup (100 g) of fine coconut flakes

½ cup (60 g) of coconut butter (purchase at fancy stores for rip-off price, or puree the heck out of another cup of coconut flakes until they become buttery)

¼ cup (60 g) of coconut oil (told ya there was a lot of coconut)

⅓ cup (43 g) of almond flour or coconut flour

½ cup (120 g) of cacao nibs

1 tablespoon (15 ml) of vanilla extract

1 tablespoon (7 g) of cinnamon

1 tablespoon (15 g) of peanut, almond, cashew, macadamia nut, or other exotic nut/seed butter

1 teaspoon (5 g) of Real Salt or other natural sea salt or Himalayan pink salt

Optional sweetener: a few drops of stevia, 1 tablespoon (15 g) of honey or maple syrup, and/or 2 tablespoons (30 ml) of lemon juice

WHAT TO DO

1. Gently heat the coconut butter, coconut oil, and any liquid sweeteners.

2. Mix the dry stuff in a large bowl, then stir in the liquid mixture.

3. Stir everything together thoroughly.

4. Form ping-pong ball sized balls with your hands, pressing hard to make the balls as firm as you can.

5. Gently place in a glass casserole dish or on a cookie sheet.

6. Refrigerate for 30-60 minutes or until they feel rock hard.

7. Store in Tupperware at room temperature and enjoy whenever you need to feel good about yourself.

Just another day for JT: Mack on balls, charge double-O's, bounce to J-Lo's and lay low.

Note: Brad's friend JT tasted Brad's Delicious White Balls for the first time, then nailed his best front-tube ride ever at Rincon in December 2018. On that day, it was pumping double overhead and so fully zoo'ed with Barns that JT almost sketched out and bounced in his Jag. However, he was so baked on the balls that he dropped in on Curren and chilled in the green room for a bit before F-Typing back to the 'Wood to party with Jenna A, Jay-Z, J-Lo, and B ('yonce). Hey. True story, brah. Shaka. Peace. Read JT's *Millennium Manifesto*. Out.

(12 balls with 1 Tbs. peanut butter, no sweetener)

MACRONUTRIENTS PER SERVING: CALORIES: 133   FAT: 13 G   CARBS: 4 G   PROTEIN: 2 G

BREAKING THE MOLDS

These are tiny frozen treats that you suck on (especially if you are trying to quit smoking, dude!). You can be creative with the content options, but the following mix is delicious and quite satiating due to the coconut oil. You need to invest in a silicone mini ice-cube tray mold; we're talking a set of three for ten bucks online or at a Bed 'N Bath or other kitchen supply store.

INGREDIENTS

½ cup (120 g) of coconut oil

2 tablespoons (30 g) of almond butter or peanut butter

1 ounce (28 g) of 85%+ dark chocolate

¼ cup (25 g) of fresh berries or pomegranate seeds

WHAT TO DO

1. Melt the coconut oil (or just open the coconut oil lid if you live in Phoenix) and carelessly pour into each ice-cube mold to fill them halfway.

2. Sloppily add a dollop of almond or peanut butter to each mold.

3. Break up the chocolate into tiny bits and add a couple bits to each mold.

4. Finish the masterpiece with a bit of berries or pomegranates.

5. Stick in the freezer for a couple of hours. Pop them out into a bowl and store in the freezer. Put some different stuff in them next time and see what happens.

COOKING TIME:
10 MINS
SERVINGS:

(12 servings with blueberries)
MACRONUTRIENTS PER SERVING: CALORIES: 112 FAT: 12 G CARBS: 1 G PROTEIN: 1 G

CHEGGZ
(CHOCOLATE EGGS)

COOKING TIME:
10 MINS
SERVINGS:
1

Chocolate is a straight up superfood. Chocolate Eggs are a great way to get more chocolate into your life through a nutrient-dense meal, without it turning into a decadent snack/dessert. Dark chocolate is rich in a flavonoid called *epicatechin,* which has been shown to be a myostatin inhibitor. This means when you consume Cheggz post-workout, you will get freakin' ripped in 23-30 days.

INGREDIENTS

5 eggs

2 tablespoons (10 g) of raw cacao powder

Cooking oil/butter (extra credit: use cacao butter)

Sea salt

Cinnamon

Cacao nibs

Nut butter (almond, peanut, or coconut)

Optional: stevia

WHAT TO DO

1. Heat a frying pan to medium with cooking oil.

2. Blend 5 eggs with 2 tablespoons (10 g) of cacao powder, salt, and cinnamon.

3. Once the pan is hot, pour in the egg and cacao blend.

4. If you're ambitious, you can try to make a crepe/omelet, but it's easy to just scramble it up.

5. Transfer the cooked eggs to a bowl.

6. Top with nut butter, cacao nibs, and more cinnamon.

Note: If it's too bitter after your first go-round, add a bit of stevia to the mixture.

(1 serving with 1 Tbs. almond butter, cacao nibs, and cooked in 1 Tbs. cacao butter)
MACRONUTRIENTS PER SERVING: CALORIES: 647   FAT: 52 G   CARBS: 21 G   PROTEIN: 37 G

Chocolate Mousse
ALA BIG GEORGE

COOKING TIME:
20 MINS TO PREP & 2-3 HOURS TO CHILL

SERVINGS:
6

This is one of the greatest dessert recipes on the planet, but it's so healthy you can eat it for breakfast. Or, for a snack after Speedgolf or a cold plunge. It's high in healthy fats and antioxidants and has almost no carbs. There are only four ingredients, so it's an easy qualifier for this book. Big George, aka Dr. Ray Sidney, perfected this recipe while getting A's at Harvard (bachelors), MIT (Ph.D.), and UC Berkeley (MBA). How about you? What you have you been doing the past 20 years? Make this recipe so you can make something out of your life. These proportions make a massive dose to feed your family or party guests.

INGREDIENTS

(Massive dose to serve family and friends)

6 eggs – get pasture-raised eggs, don't be a loser with regular eggs

10 ounces (284 g) of 85%+ dark chocolate; most bars are 3.5 ounces, so use 3 bars while eating a few squares. Go 85% or higher. Get a quality bean-to-bar product like Eco Dark, or budget with Trader Joe's 85% dark product

4 ounces (113 g) butter – that's half of a Kerrygold bar or a full traditional stick

WHAT TO DO

1. Melt the chocolate and butter together in a double boiler. A double boiler is stacking two pots, with the lower pot full of water and the top pot filled with ingredients. Do it this way because you can't melt chocolate directly, it's too sensitive. Use medium-low heat, stir frequently, and remove from the heat when melted.

2. Separate the eggs using a big bowl for whites and smaller bowl for yolks. Mix 'em both up.

3. Whip the whites with an eggbeater or a fancy whip cream machine thing until they're fluffy and dry. Pretty cool how they fluff up huh?! I think chicks put this on their face, not sure…

4. Stir the yolks into the melted chocolate and butter.

5. Fold the yolk/chocolate/butter mixture into the whites, stirring gently. Mix it all up gently.

6. Pour into a glass* tupperware and refrigerate for a few hours. Serve with homemade whipped cream on top if you want.

Plasticware will give you erectile dysfunction and eventually cancer. Use glass, dude!

(6 SERVINGS WITH 3 3.5-OUNCE CHOCOLATE BARS)
MACRONUTRIENTS PER SERVING: CALORIES: 523 FAT: 46 G CARBS: 10 G PROTEIN: 11 G

COCONUT & PECAN CRUSTED CHICKEN TENDERS

COOKING TIME: **30 MINS** SERVINGS: **8**

We know that this recipe uses a few bowls and might take a little longer to clean up, but did you read the title? Coconut & Pecan Crusted Chicken Tenders. Mmm. It's worth it, folks.

INGREDIENTS

1 pound (454 g) of chicken tenders

1 cup (100 g) of dried coconut

1 cup (125 g) pecans

Sea salt, pepper & garlic powder

½ teaspoon (3 g) cayenne pepper

2 eggs

WHAT TO DO

1. Pat dry your chicken tenders with a paper towel and throw the towel away to avoid spreading salmonella.

2. Preheat your oven to 400F (204C).

3. Run dried coconut, pecans, a sprinkle of sea salt, pepper and garlic powder, and cayenne powder in a food processor until everything is the same size and resembles a nutty flour.

4. Crack eggs in a shallow bowl and whisk.

5. Coat each chicken tender in egg and then dredge it in the coconut mixture.

6. Place on a baking tray lined with parchment paper and bake for about 20 minutes, flipping after 10 minutes.

7. Keep an eye on your tenders to ensure the crust doesn't burn, as some ovens run hotter than others!

MACRONUTRIENTS PER SERVING: CALORIES: 201 FAT: 24 G CARBS: 7 G PROTEIN: 15 G

Coconut
ICE CREAM

Some muppets say that they can't do keto because they can't live without their ice cream. In with this simple recipe, out with that excuse!

INGREDIENTS

2 cups (480 ml) of unsweetened, full-fat coconut milk

½ teaspoon (2.5 g) of Himalayan salt or natural sea salt

1 tablespoon (15 ml) of pure vanilla extract

Optional

Sweetener: several drops or one small packet of stevia. Or choose another sweetener like monk fruit, xylitol, or erythritol

Flavoring ingredients: crushed berries, lemon or lime juice, fine bits of ginger, shredded or ground coconut, cacao nibs or cocoa powder, or peanut or almond butter

WHAT TO DO

1. In a large bowl, mix the coconut milk, salt, vanilla, sweetener, and any flavors.

2. If you have a hand or electric ice cream maker, process as directed. If not, freeze mixture in ice cube trays, then drop the frozen cubes into a food processor or Blendtec blender.

3. Enjoy immediately, as it's difficult to preserve perfect ice cream texture without the gums, stabilizers, carrageenan, soy lecithin, industrial seed oils, and other shit found in Ben & Jerry's (including, shockingly, the villainous glyphosate, aka Roundup weed killer). If you store some of the ice cream cubes, just go through the blending process again to achieve some freshness.

(4 servings, no sweetener or toppings)
MACRONUTRIENTS PER SERVING: CALORIES: 189 FAT: 18 G CARBS: 2 G PROTEIN: 0 G

Creamiest
ORANGE CRÈME
CHIA PUDDING

Remember the ice cream with the orange and vanilla squares throughout it? No? Oh, maybe that's because it's no longer being made and now you have an idea of how old we are. Or, it's because you're making this chia pudding now, and all other orange crème treats have been forgotten. We think it might be a bit of both.

INGREDIENTS

1 cup (240 g) coconut yogurt

1 tablespoon (10 g) chia seeds

1 teaspoon (5 g) vanilla bean powder

1 tablespoon (6 g) orange zest

WHAT TO DO

1. Thoroughly mix chia seeds in plain coconut yogurt (use a yogurt with very few ingredients, your local health food shop should have a few options).

2. Mix in about 1 teaspoon (5 g) of vanilla bean powder (you can purchase this on Amazon, it will transform this recipe and any smoothie recipe) and orange zest.

3. Allow to set in the fridge for at least 30 minutes before serving with optional peeled orange slices.

MACRONUTRIENTS PER SERVING: CALORIES: 267 FAT: 26 G CARBS: 8 G PROTEIN: 5 G

EGGPLANT
TAHINI DIP

COOKING TIME:
1-2 HOURS TO PREP, 40 MINS
SERVINGS:
8

Eggplant and tahini blended together make for a delicious dip for veggies, meats, and seafoods. Amp up the flavor by adding some cumin powder or fresh cilantro or feta cheese as a garnish to this dip.

INGREDIENTS

1 medium (250 g) eggplant

Sea salt & pepper

2 tablespoons (30 g) tahini

3 garlic cloves

¼ cup (60 ml) olive oil

1 teaspoon (2 g) smoked paprika

WHAT TO DO

1. Remove the inedible top and end pieces of the eggplant and throw away.

2. Slice the eggplant in 2" discs and allow to "sweat" by placing on a cooling rack for an hour or two. You'll see its water releasing (this is it "sweating") and you can simply wipe it dry with a cloth.

3. When the eggplant has released some of its water, preheat the oven to 400 degrees F (204 C).

4. Roast the eggplant on a baking tray lined with parchment paper and a sprinkle of sea salt and pepper until its soft and browned, about 35–30 minutes. You can flip halfway through if you like.

5. When it's done, remove from the oven and place in a blender or food processor with tahini and garlic cloves.

6. Blend until very creamy, adding olive oil to really thicken it up.

7. Serve immediately with a sprinkle of smoked paprika (and fresh parsley to impress your friends) to dip in veggies or over meats or serve it cold by chilling it in the fridge for a few hours before enjoying.

MACRONUTRIENTS PER SERVING: CALORIES: 92 FAT: 13 G CARBS: 3 G PROTEIN: 1 G

IT'S NOT INFLAMMATORY
→ DIP

Check the labels for many of the pre-made dips from the market....yeah, we're crying, too. But we've stopped because we started making our own and realized it was easy to do. And when we're using recipes like this one, our bodies and brains are thanking us for having ditched the junk in favor of good old-fashioned food.

INGREDIENTS

1 cup (240 g) Primal Kitchen Avocado Oil Mayo

Sea salt, pepper & garlic powder

1 tablespoon (7 g) dried turmeric powder

2 tablespoons (30 g) hot sauce

1 whole scallion

WHAT TO DO

1. Thoroughly mix mayonnaise, sea salt, garlic powder, pepper, and turmeric powder in a bowl.

2. Add hot sauce (less if you like less heat, more if you like your mouth burning) and a minced scallion. Mix well.

3. Serve with veggies or with meats and seafood.

COOKING TIME: **5 MINS**
SERVINGS: **8**

MACRONUTRIENTS PER SERVING: CALORIES: 203   FAT: 24 G   CARBS: 1 G   PROTEIN: 0 G

KETO
CHEESECAKE

COOKING TIME:
1 HR 40 MINS
SERVINGS:
ABOUT 7

INGREDIENTS

Cheesecake

16 ounces (454 g) of organic cream cheese

2 tablespoons (30 ml) of pure vanilla extract

2 teaspoons (10 ml) of lemon juice

2 teaspoons (10 g) of natural salt

2 eggs

Sweetener: ¼ cup (84 g) of stevia and/or 2 tablespoons (30 g) of honey

Crust

1 cup (100 g) of almond or coconut flour

4 tablespoons (60 g) of butter

1-2 tablespoons (15-30 g) of stevia

1 tablespoon (15 ml) of vanilla extract

Chocolate Crunch Topping

3.5-ounce (100 g) bar of 85%+ dark chocolate

Pureed nuts

Coconut flakes

If you're a cheesecake fan, you will quickly habituate to this less sweet but just as savory offering as a traditional cheesecake. Keto cheesecake is all the rage, having been designated by *Food & Wine* magazine as one of the top 5 foods the Internet was most obsessed with in 2018 and as reported by two of our favorite health and fitness experts and Cool Dudes Ben Greenfield (BenGreenfieldfitness.com) and Brock Armstrong (GetFitGuy.com) on a 2019 *Ben Greenfield Fitness* podcast. Another *Food & Wine* survey reported that males listing "keto cheesecake" on their online dating profiles got 10% more swipes and likes than males who didn't write keto cheesecake anywhere. If you're ready to get cooler as a dude, try this recipe. Every day.

WHAT TO DO

1. First, use quality ingredients. Ben Greenfield says cheap vanilla is extracted from beaver anus. No kidding, he said that, and Ben is always right. Get organic cream cheese to steer clear of hormones and antibiotics in conventional dairy. If you are tightly restricting carbs, use stevia, or throw in some honey if you're not stressed about it.

2. Choose between Instant Pot **or** oven instructions. Combine all ingredients in a large bowl and mix thoroughly with a machine mixer on low speed.

CONTINUED >>

COOKING – INSTANT POT

1. Use a round glass bowl or springform pan that can fit inside the Instant Pot.

2. Pour mixture into the bowl and cover carefully with aluminum foil.

3. Pour two cups (480 ml) of water into the Instant Pot stainless steel pot, then put the cheesecake bowl onto the rack. Or buy the Instant Pot steamer basket accessory, which is way better than the flimsy rack that comes with the Instant Pot.

4. Cook on high pressure for 25 minutes. Let pressure naturally disperse for about 15 minutes, then remove from the pot.

COOKING – OVEN

1. Preheat to 350F (175C). Use a springform pan ($10-$20 online) or a round glass or ceramic bakeware.

2. Place mixture in springform pan, then cover with aluminum foil.

Almond Flour Crust

1. Mix the almond flour, vanilla, and sweetener and press into the bottom of the springform pan.

2. Bake for 10 minutes or until crust turns a little darker gold, then cool for 10 minutes.

3. Pour the cheesecake filling mixture into the pan and smooth out the top with your hand (just kidding, use a spatula).

4. Bake at 350F (175C) for 50 minutes. Make sure the middle is almost firm, but not quite.

5. Cool for 10 minutes, then apply the chocolate crunch topping. Then, refrigerate for several hours before removing from springform pan and cutting slices to enjoy.

Chocolate Crunch Topping

1. Maybe the best part if you nail this! Puree ¼ to ½ cup (30-60 g) of macadamia nuts or assorted nuts. Add 2-3 tablespoons (6-12 g) of fine coconut flakes.

2. Melt a 3.5-ounce (100 g) chocolate bar plus one tablespoon (15 g) of coconut oil in a double broiler pan or microwave.

3. Mix the nuts and coconut into the melted chocolate, then drizzle carefully across the top of the cheesecake.

4. Refrigerate the cheesecake for 30-60 minutes until the crust feels hard, then serve.

(7 SERVINGS, USED THE HIGHER END OF ALL INGREDIENT SUGGESTIONS)
MACRONUTRIENTS PER SERVING: CALORIES: 556 FAT: 49 G CARBS: 16 G PROTEIN: 12 G

Mascarpone Mousse with
TOP SECRET LEMON VANILLA INFUSION

COOKING TIME:
15 MINS TO CHILL BOWL & 5 MINS TO MIX
SERVINGS: **8**

This is the ultimate dessert foundation to serve on top of or with anything. Fresh pomegranate seeds or berries is the baseline fantastic option to serve with. Experimental dudes might enjoy garnishing with finely chopped nuts, the innards of Brad's Delicious White Balls (page 170), the crumbles from Stu Can't Stop Bark (page 192), or a drizzle of Perfect Keto's incredible multi-nut-with-MCT-oil keto butter or any other nut butter. Make a double batch and it will keep for about a week. It's so low in sugar you can eat it for breakfast.

INGREDIENTS

2 8-ounce (454 g) tubs of Mascarpone cheese: found in weird little tubs instead of bar-shaped cheese, maybe even in a different grocery section, just ask a cute or knowledgeable looking clerk

1 pint (480 ml) of organic heavy cream

½ to 1 lemon

1 tablespoon (15 ml) of vanilla extract

Optional: A few drops of stevia.

Note: The infusion really adds a kick to the preparation, but food snobs will frown upon it because you're supposed to use a shit ton of sugar instead.

WHAT TO DO

1. Put the attachment thingies from your handheld mix blender, or bad ass countertop mixer, into the freezer along with a deep bowl that you will use to blend to pre-cool them.

2. Once nicely chilled, remove the bowl and dump the ingredients in there and mix until everything is combined. Be careful not to overdo the stevia, realizing that this is a rich dessert, not a sweet one.

MACRONUTRIENTS PER SERVING: CALORIES: 452 FAT: 46 G CARBS: 3 G PROTEIN: 1 G

Prosciutto doesn't get as much fame as bacon, but you'll be wondering why when you start using it more, such as in this recipe for prosciutto-wrapped asparagus. Some people find the fatty ends of it a bit chewy, so tear those off if that is your preference.

PROSCIUTTO-WRAPPED ASPARAGUS

INGREDIENTS

8 ounces (227 g) of sliced prosciutto

1 pound (454 g) asparagus

Sea salt and pepper

Parsley

WHAT TO DO

1. Chop the rough ends of the asparagus off and throw away.

2. You can steam the asparagus for 5 minutes if you prefer it soft or keep it raw if you like a nice crunch.

3. Place a piece of asparagus on top of a piece of prosciutto.

4. Sprinkle with sea salt (optional since the prosciutto is already pretty salty), pepper, and a sprig of parsley.

5. Wrap the prosciutto tightly around the asparagus and parsley and serve on a platter at your next shindig.

COOKING TIME: **10 MINS** SERVINGS: **4**

MACRONUTRIENTS PER SERVING: CALORIES: 163 FAT: 8 G CARBS: 4 G PROTEIN: 18 G

SMOKED TURKEY ROLL-UPS

COOKING TIME:
10 MINS
SERVINGS:
2

Ok, you don't have to use smoked turkey. You can use oven–roasted. You could even use another deli meat, we promise, mums the word! These roll-ups offer all the flavor of your favorite sammie, without the insulin spike, and we really like that around here.

INGREDIENTS

1 6-ounce (170 g) package of smoked deli turkey

1 medium (150 g) avocado

6 slices of bacon

4 tablespoons (28 g) sun-dried tomatoes

Parsley

WHAT TO DO

1. Cook bacon and set aside, crumbling when it has cooled.

2. Place turkey slices on a cutting board and place sliced avocado, crumbled bacon, and a couple pieces of sun-dried tomatoes and parsley on each center.

3. Carefully roll up and secure with a toothpick, if needed.

4. Serve on a platter and be everyone's favorite at the party.

MACRONUTRIENTS PER SERVING: CALORIES: 332   FAT: 23 G   CARBS: 6 G   PROTEIN: 26 G

STU CAN'T STOP
B·A·R·K

This dark chocolate macadamia nut bark is a fabulous snack or dessert treat. Named after Brad's dog Stu, who sometimes barks too much, and also because it's so good that you can't stop eating it! You'll get mobbed at parties (like Brad) if you bring this offering. Full keto—very low sugar, high antioxidant, and highly nutritious.

COOKING TIME:
20 MINS TO PREP & 1-2 HRS TO CHILL
SERVINGS:
8

INGREDIENTS

4 bars (3.5 oz/400 g – typical size) of 85%+ dark chocolate. Get a quality bean-to-bar brand like Eco Dark 85% or 90%, or go budget-friendly with Trader Joe's Dark Chocolate Lovers 85% dark

2 tablespoons (30 g) of coconut oil

1 cup (125 g) of macadamia nuts or other nuts, pureed in Cuisinart, Ninja food chopper, or other mini-blender. Or, chop with a small knife for two hours if you're lame

Optional: Peanut or almond butter to smear a layer in the middle of the mixture, ¼ to ½ cup (25-50 g) finely shredded coconut flakes or puree bigger flakes in a blender, coconut butter to sprinkle on top at the end, sea salt to sprinkle on top at the end

WHAT TO DO

1. Boil water in a double boiler (pot of water boiling with a pot stacked on top and lidded).

2. Rip apart the chocolate bars with your bare hands while still in the box. Like a man. Then, open the boxes and wrappers and dump half of the chocolate bits into top pot. If bars have a foil wrapper, be careful to clear the foil bits. Add the coconut oil. Melt on low–medium heat, stirring regularly until mixture is smooth.

3. In a big mixing bowl, mix the pureed nuts and the other half of the chocolate bits that you broke apart by hand like a man. Don't worry about making them super small, just sprinkle the random-sized chunks into the bowl.

4. Pour the melted chocolate/coconut oil mixture into bowl and stir everything together well.

5. Get a casserole dish and spread the mixture thinly across the dish. Drizzle the nut butter across half of the mixture, then spread the rest of the chocolate mix in. Sprinkle flecks of coconut butter across the top. Finish with a sprinkle of salt across the top.

6. Refrigerate or freeze for 1-2 hours until it feels rock hard. Take it out and let it sit for 5-10 minutes until it gives a bit to a knife. Cut into chunks, ideally with a "baker's blade" or "dough scraper" that has a straight edge. Or, cut carefully with a strong knife.

7. Store in the refrigerator because the bark softens and eventually will melt, even at room temperature.

(8 SERVINGS, NO TOPPINGS)
MACRONUTRIENTS PER SERVING: CALORIES: 442 FAT: 41 G CARBS: 11 G PROTEIN: 6 G

SUN-DRIED TOMATO & WALNUT DIP

If you like a dip bursting with flavor with a bunch of texture, this is the dip you've been waiting for! We used dried basil, but by all means, use fresh if you have it.

INGREDIENTS

1 8.1-ounce (241 g) jar of sun-dried tomatoes packed in olive oil

1 cup (125 g) walnuts

Sea salt & pepper

2 garlic cloves

1 tablespoon (2 g) dried basil

1 tablespoon (15 ml) lemon juice

WHAT TO DO

1. Place entire jar of sun-dried tomatoes in a food processor with chopped walnuts, garlic clove, lemon juice, and a big sprinkle of sea salt and pepper.

2. Pulse until everything is minced, scraping down the sides of the processor bowl as needed.

3. Serve with veggies and meats or with fried eggs.

COOKING TIME:
10 MINUTES
SERVINGS:
8

MACRONUTRIENTS PER SERVING: CALORIES: 123 FAT: 10 G CARBS: 8 G PROTEIN: 3 G

WALNUT HERB CHEESE LOG

This is the type of recipe that looks like it was more involved than it really was to prepare, meaning, make it for a party when you're looking to make a good impression. Just put it on a fancy platter and serve with in-season veggies.

INGREDIENTS

1 16-ounce (454 g) goat cheese log

1 cup (125 g) chopped walnuts

Parsley & scallion

Sea salt & pepper

1 tablespoon (3 g) dried dill

WHAT TO DO

1. Mince parsley and scallion (and walnuts if they aren't already in very small pieces) and toss in a bowl with a big sprinkle of sea salt and pepper.

2. Pour onto a flat surface (parchment paper works great) and roll goat cheese in it until the cheese is completely covered by walnuts and herbs.

3. Serve on a platter with veggies such as sliced cucumber, red peppers, or radish.

COOKING TIME:
5 MINUTES
MAKES:
**1 POUND OR
16 SERVINGS**

MACRONUTRIENTS PER SERVING: CALORIES: 124   FAT: 11 G   CARBS: 1 G   PROTEIN: 6 G

SMOOTHIES & BEVER-AGES

BERRY
SMOOTHIE

COOKING TIME:
10 MINS
SERVINGS:
1

There's a lot of smoothies out there with greens in them, and if they weird you out even a little, we think this recipe will expand all you thought about blended greens tasting gross. Use fresh or frozen spinach and berries and play around with different protein powders, if using those are your thing.

INGREDIENTS

1 cup (240 ml) almond milk

¼ cup (25 g) blueberries

2 cups (60 g) spinach

Sea salt

2 tablespoons (30 g) almond butter

Collagen powder or protein powder (or both)

Ice cubes

WHAT TO DO

1. Blend all ingredients until very creamy.

2. For a colder, frothier smoothie, add about 4 ice cubes when blending.

3. Serve immediately.

MACRONUTRIENTS PER SERVING: CALORIES: 304 FAT: 22 G CARBS: 15 G PROTEIN: 20 G

CAULIFLOWER
SMOOTHIE BOWL

COOKING TIME:
10 MINS
SERVINGS:
1

Frozen cauliflower rice is now an easy-to-find staple at nearly any grocery store. It's bland taste and granular nature makes it an excellent base for a nutrient-dense and super-thick smoothie bowl. That's right, many Cool Dudes can drink a regular old smoothie, but if you want your life to break through to the next level, consider making smoothies so thick that you have to eat them out of a bowl.

INGREDIENTS

Base

1 scoop (20 g) of vanilla flavored whey protein

1 raw egg

1 16-ounce bag (454 g) of frozen cauliflower rice

1 tablespoon (15 g) of nut butter

¼ cup (60 ml) of water

Sea salt

Cinnamon

Optional: glucomannan powder

Toppings

Cacao nibs

Nuts

Coconut flakes

WHAT TO DO

1. Add ¼ cup (60 ml) of water, the raw egg, whey protein, and sea salt to a blender and start blending on low/slow.

2. Slowly start pouring in the cauliflower rice. The goal is to make the smoothie as big and as thick as possible so start slowly and keep adding as much cauliflower rice as possible. You may need to help stir with a spoon if the blender gets stuck.

3. Add in the nut butter towards the end. If you're having trouble reaching a desirable texture, add in a few pinches of glucomannan powder.

4. Empty into a big bowl and top with cacao nibs, nuts, coconut flakes, and cinnamon.

(1 serving with 3 ounces cauliflower rice, 1 Tbs. almond butter, 1 Tbs. each almonds, cacao nibs & dried coconut)
MACRONUTRIENTS PER SERVING: CALORIES: 599   FAT: 41 G   CARBS: 41 G   PROTEIN: 23 G

COOKING TIME:
10 MINS TO PREP & 11-14 DAYS TO FERMENT

MAKES:
SEVERAL 1-CUP (240 ML) SERVINGS

HOMEMADE KOMBUCHA WITH WHITE BALLS

We only said "white balls" so you would laugh for a second time after making Brad's Delicious White Balls with coconut products and nut butter, but go ahead and enjoy them with your kombucha. Kombucha is packed with probiotics to promote healthy intestinal function. After a string of surgeries and heavy antibiotic use in 2015, Brad credits mass consumption of kombucha for finally healing his gut after a couple years of complaints, imperfections, and getting sick on four consecutive visits to Mexico.

Dudes have some objections with store-bought kombucha that will inspire you to make your own: First, it's butt naked expensive—$3.25 for a typical 16-ounce container is 26 bucks a gallon! Second, the exotic flavors they offer have been sweetened and carbonated inauthentically in post-production to appeal to a soda-crazed public. Read some of the labels and you will see up to 20 grams of carbohydrates in a 16-ounce bottle. This is not keto-friendly!

Making your own kombucha is super fun because you are presiding over a living breathing organism, much like a snobby vinter, hippie pot grower, or beet farmer on a long running sitcom. There is something extra rewarding about drinking something you created from an entirely different starting product of super sweet black tea. So let's get to it! First step is to find a friend who can give you a SCOBY—a Symbiotic Culture Of Bacteria and Yeast. Anyone who makes kombucha can help, because a SCOBY baby is hatched upon completion of every batch. Think deeply about who the coolest people in your *Rolodex* (that's a nickname for "Smartphone contacts that are also housed in the cloud") are, and see if they are in the kombucha game. If you strike out, just head to the nearest natural foods market and chat up the coolest looking clerk and they will lead you to someone, somewhere who can score you a SCOBY. The SCOBY is what makes it all happen. The SCOBY literally eats the sugar and caffeine from the sweet tea and turns it into kombucha after a 11-14 day fermentation period.

INGREDIENTS

1 SCOBY in 1-2 cups of its own liquid (kombucha)

8 bags of black tea: fully caffeinated hard stuff, no fooling around

1 cup (200 g) of organic sugar. No fooling around, but get organic for maximum purity

2 one-gallon glass jars and 4 quart jars (or 2 half-gallon jars)

WHAT TO DO

1. Put the SCOBY and the kombucha it came with into one of the gallon jars.

2. In the other jar, fill with water almost to the top, brew the tea all the way, then add the sugar and stir well.

3. When the tea cools, remove bags (squeeze every last drop out of the bags, it's fun and makes for the strongest tea), then pour the SCOBY and kombucha into the cooled tea.

4. Cover the lid with a cheesecloth or other breathable mesh, gauze-like cloth, and rubber band into position. You want the SCOBY to breathe but you want to keep out bugs and debris.

5. Mark the date on the glass with a sticky note and then store in a warm dry place away from direct sunlight. Brew for at least 11 days and up to 14.

6. Sneak spoonful tastes over time and you will notice a shift from the ultra-sweet black tea to a more sour, vinegar-like unflavored kombucha. In fact, your gallon of kombucha starts with 1 cup (200 g) of sugar and ferments down 50-70 percent to between 2.5 to 6 grams per cup (240 ml) of low-glycemic sugar. Since Brad drinks large quantities and wants to remain a Cool Keto Dude, he cuts the kombucha with one-half to two-thirds carbonated water. So, he kinda gets his soda fix just like the people buying store-bought kombucha, but he saves a lot of cash.

Note: The creativity kicks in after this first fermentation is complete. Relocate the SCOBY and two cups (480 ml) of liquid into the spare gallon jar, then pour the kombucha into smaller containers to let the flavoring begin. Brad likes to use the giant one-liter kombucha jars from the store, or you can get several quart jars to experiment with flavorings. Add desired flavoring from the list below, seal the lid, and commence the second fermentation lasting around 3 days. Again, in a warm spot away from direct sunlight. After three days, you will have a bit of carbonation and the distinct flavoring on top of the plain kombucha base from the first fermentation.

SECOND FERMENTATION FLAVORING OPTIONS

- **Freshly squeezed lemons and limes**

- **Fruit flavored herbal tea bags**
  Good Earth has some fantastic options. *Sweet & Spicy Original* is the best tea on the planet. The 4-flavor variety packs on Amazon offer fantastic variety.

- **Jalapeño pepper**
  Slice into quarters and drop in 2-4 slices. Leaving the seeds in will add a further kick.

- **Diced ginger root**
  The end product will taste like ginger ale, according to Cool Dude and health enthusiast David Lapp. Drop in some fresh mint from the garden for extra credit.

- **Fresh berries**
  Drop in a handful.

- **Dried fruit—mangoes, apricots**
  Knock yourself out.

- **Fruit juice**
  Remember the second fermentation will consume much of the sugar from the juice, as happened during the first fermentation.

MACRONUTRIENTS PER SERVING: CALORIES: 25 FAT: 0 G CARBS: 6 G PROTEIN: 0 G

On really hot days, you might just want a pink smoothie to remind you of slushies and ice cream and things you don't eat anymore now that you're Keto. Play around with different protein powders until you've found one that you would drive across town for.

RASPBERRY *BENDER*

INGREDIENTS

1 cup (125 g) frozen raspberries

1 cup (240 ml) water

2 scoops (40 g) vanilla pea protein powder (just a suggestion)

Collagen powder

1 tablespoon (15 ml) MCT oil

Sea salt

WHAT TO DO

1. Blend about a cup (125 g) of frozen raspberries with a cup of water, a serving of protein powder, collagen, MCT oil, and a pinch of sea salt.

2. Serve immediately. You can add cinnamon or almond butter (or both) to jazz this smoothie up.

COOKING TIME:
5 MINS
SERVINGS:
1

MACRONUTRIENTS PER SERVING: CALORIES: 304 FAT: 22 G CARBS: 15 G PROTEIN: 20 G

SUPER NUTRITION MORNING GREEN SMOOTHIE

(VIRAL YOUTUBE VERSION)

This recipe made Brad (host) and Brian (cinematographer) world famous when a YouTube video of the same name went viral with over 800 views. It is inspired by two smart and handsome nutritional consultants and progressive health leaders, Chris Kelly and Dr. Tommy Wood of NourishBalanceThrive.com. While supportive of the ketogenic movement, Kelly and Wood also advocate for high consumption of nutrient-dense foods, especially for athletes. This macronutrient-balanced smoothie gives you a concentrated dose of antioxidants, vitamins, minerals, and specialized performance agents. For athletic keto enthusiasts, fasting till lunch is great at times, and starting the day with a powerhouse smoothie is great at times.

The key to smoothie success is having readily available bags of mixed produce in your freezer. Anytime produce is getting near spoiling or you have discards from a veggie stir fry meal, throw them into the freezer bags. Start out with a couple large Ziploc bags with baseline items of spinach, kale, chopped beets, a small ratio of berries, and peeled and frozen green bananas (for resistant starch). Also consider including bok choy, celery, chard, cucumber, and, as Dr. Tommy Wood adds, "discards from last night's veggie stir fry." A nationwide survey reported that males listing "green smoothie" on their online dating profiles got 10 percent more swipes and likes than males who don't drink smoothies.

INGREDIENTS

2 cups (480 ml) of unsweetened, full-fat non-dairy milk (coconut, almond, etc.)

2 big handfuls of pre-frozen mixed greens and veggies. Mix together in large Ziploc bag, then freeze: kale, spinach, celery, cucumber, beets, green banana, and a small ratio of frozen berries

2 scoops (40 g) of whey protein power or Primal Fuel meal replacement powder

1 tablespoon (15 ml) of MCT (medium chain triglyceride) oil (Mickey T8 brand online is good)

1 teaspoon (5 g) of performance agents such as creatine, glutamine, L-carnitine

Capsules of important stuff you are taking like Vitamin D and Male Optimization Formula with Organs (MOFO) from AncestralSupplements.com/mofo

2 teaspoons (10 g) of Real Salt or other high-quality mineral salt

Optional flavoring: vanilla, cinnamon, half a lemon (surprisingly interesting flavor option for the adventurous)

WHAT TO DO

1. Add the ingredients in the following order to make sure the blender can succeed: liquids, powders, then solids such as produce.

2. Pour in a large glass and enjoy.

COOKING TIME:
10 MINS
SERVINGS:
1

(1 serving with 1 cup spinach, 1 celery stalk, ½ cup cucumber, ¼ cup berries, Primal Fuel powder, 1 tsp. creatine)
MACRONUTRIENTS PER SERVING: CALORIES: 417   FAT: 28 G   CARBS: 19 G   PROTEIN: 24 G

INDEX

C